THE DISTANT SHORE

MORE IRISH STORIES
FROM THE EDGE OF DEATH

COLM KEANE

CAPEL
ISLAND

First published in Ireland in 2010

by

CAPEL ISLAND PRESS
36 Raheen Park, Bray,
County Wicklow, Ireland

ISBN 978-0-9559133-2-7

Printed by ColourBooks Ltd, Dublin
Typesetting and cover design by Typeform Ltd

For Seán

COLM KEANE'S 20 books include the number one bestsellers *Going Home: Irish Stories From The Edge Of Death*, *Padre Pio: The Irish Connection* and *Nervous Breakdown*. He is a graduate of Trinity College, Dublin, and Georgetown University, Washington DC. As a broadcaster, he won a Jacob's Award and a Glaxo Fellowship for European Science Writers. His nine chart bestsellers include *The Jobs Crisis*, *Death And Dying* and *The Stress File*.

CONTENTS

All goes onward and outward, nothing collapses,
And to die is different from what any one supposed,
And luckier.

Song Of Myself, Walt Whitman (1819 – 1892)

INTRODUCTION

This book was inspired by the extraordinary response to the publication of *Going Home* in October 2009. National and local newspapers gave it huge coverage. So did radio and TV. Large numbers of people contacted me through radio programmes or by letter. *Going Home* went to number one and stayed in the bestseller list from October through March.

I wasn't surprised. Death, after all, is a topic close to us all. Nothing is more fundamental. Its shadow is always there. Parents, husbands, wives, children, friends die, leaving us lost, bewildered and bereft. We die ourselves, some earlier than others, most of us peacefully while more struggle with discomfort and pain.

Death strikes at any time, at any age, unexpectedly, cruelly and with brutal finality. I have experienced it in my own life with the passing away of parents, brothers, friends and other immediate family. It is bewildering, moving, distressing and characterised by dashed hopes, shattered dreams, wistful memories and promise lost.

Nothing, however, prepared me for the rollercoaster of intense emotion that followed the publication of *Going Home*. I received numerous letters, phone calls, emails and other communications from all corners of Ireland – from Donegal to Wexford, from Antrim to Kerry. They also came from abroad. People sought me out to relate intimate details of lives curtailed and people departed, some with uplifting messages, others with messages coloured by despair.

Their stories, on many occasions, contained heartbreaking images of tragedy and loss. People spoke of the deaths of their young children, of the passing away of their parents, husbands and wives, of sadness and guilt, of grief beyond anything I had ever heard of before. They revealed the sorrow of words unspoken, of emotions unexpressed, of boxed-in feelings. Many of their stories had been bottled up for decades – one for 50 years. Sometimes I wondered how they could face the light of day.

There was brightness too – that inexplicable, indescribable resource people possess, which helps them to rise above tragedy and grief. Their inner strength was invincible, unconquerable, indomitable and wonderful to behold. There were times when I emerged from conversations with my emotions in shreds. Yet it was comforting to know that many others had shared the experience of trauma surrounding death – it was even more consoling to know that they had risen up from despair and endured.

Their stories, however, involved much more than that. Many revealed extraordinary knowledge of the 'other side'. There were some who had, however briefly, died – following heart attacks and road accidents, from illness and disease. They described their vivid near-death experiences involving tunnels, bright lights and encounters with a 'superior being'. Others told me of parents, sisters, brothers who reappeared in visions after they died. More told me of forewarnings they had of future events.

What amazed me was how genuine, ordinary, warm and engaging all these people were. These were not cranks or fantasists spinning tall yarns or relating whimsical tales. On the contrary, they were level-headed, sane, sensible people, clear and articulate, and certain of the stories they told and the pictures they painted. They were, if my more than 30 years as a journalist is anything to go by, describing honest, real experiences from the edge of death.

It has been a genuine privilege and honour to record their stories. It has been a revelation, too, to at least partially unlock the key to the afterlife and to understand what happens when we die. 'I must go in, the fog is rising,' the poet Emily Dickinson said with her last breath. Somehow, I feel, the fog has risen for me. In the following pages I want to share what I saw with you.

Colm Keane

INTO THE LIGHT

In early summer 2009 I had a most interesting conversation with a woman named Monica, who comes from County Limerick. She contacted me having heard that I was writing a book about near-death experiences. She wanted to tell me her story. Like so many others I spoke to at that time, she was purposeful, resolute and unwavering in what she wanted to say.

By that stage I had interviewed about a dozen people who had 'seen the light'. I was already able to predict the pattern – the departure from the body, the sense of calmness and tranquillity, the bright light at the end of a dark tunnel, the border or boundary, the meeting with deceased family and friends, the encounter with a superior being, the life review and the decision to either cross over or come back.

But Monica's contribution was very different. There was something much more intense about the point she wanted to make. She repeatedly emphasised the sheer magnificence of where she had been. The peace and serenity, she told me, were amazing. The sense of warmth and comfort were unknown on earth. It was as if she was describing bliss – that feeling of perfect, spine-tingling happiness that we normally associate with something exceptional, unprecedented or unparalleled.

I listened as Monica struggled to find words – any words – that might help me understand the dramatic intensity of what she had been through. 'When I am near a person that is dying now, I almost envy the beautiful experience that is awaiting them,' she told me. She added: 'I recently knew a priest who died and I just gave him a hug and said, "Be happy. Where you are going, you wouldn't want to come back."' She went further: 'I never cry for a person that is dead. It's a new beginning and they wouldn't want to return.'

How could anyone, I wondered, be moved so profoundly? How could anything touch a person so much? Do sensations as intense as this really exist? 'The experience has changed my life,' Monica reflected. 'It lives on with me and hopefully has made me a more compassionate, caring person. I know that someday everything I do and say in this life will be reviewed by me again when I leave this world for good and my aim is to get to heaven.'

Since that inspiring conversation, which was featured in *Going Home*, many more people have described to me similar feelings of wonderment experienced on their journeys to the afterlife. Although few could match Monica's breathless amazement, words such as 'peace', 'calm', 'tranquil', 'serene', 'beautiful' and 'magnificent' still figured prominently in their conversations. This was a consistent feature throughout *Going Home*. Nothing has changed in *The Distant Shore*.

As you will see in this book, it is the sheer warmth of the experience – the feeling of happiness, joy, peace and contentment – that characterises, more than anything else, what people feel at the edge of death. Almost everyone reports it. It is the overriding force that prompts them to want to continue with their journeys. It is the principal reason why they look forward to setting out once again for the other side.

In one story related later in this book, Roisin, from County Wicklow, describes this sensation of ecstasy: 'It was like every part of my being was overwhelmed with bliss. It was a state beyond the mind, beyond happiness or joy. I felt great serenity, peace, love, harmony, calmness and oneness. This was a whole new dimension to anything I had ever been familiar with before.'

In another story featured later, Charles, from County Roscommon, explains: 'I felt very warm, cosy and peaceful. I couldn't describe the feeling of peace, it was so profound. There was no pain. I had no fear, none whatsoever.' Ann, from Connemara, adds: 'There was no discomfort. I felt calm and at peace. I just felt there was something good waiting for me where I was going. It was somewhere peaceful and comforting. It was like I was going home.'

One of the primary attractions of 'going home', of course, is the meeting – or reunion – with deceased relatives and friends. Once the 'soul', 'spirit', 'mind' or 'consciousness' leaves the body, it normally travels through a tunnel and heads for a distant bright light. The encounter usually occurs soon after, with the deceased coming forward in welcome. Since time immemorial, stories have been told of joyous reconciliations with former loved ones at the gates of heaven. Those who experience near-death know they exist.

The deceased invariably stand on the far side of the dividing line between living and dying, between life and death. This border or boundary is often a bridge, river or lake. Sometimes it is a curtain or veil. Other times it is the light. Beyond are those who have died. Approaching are those about to cross over. Had those who are approaching made it across, they wouldn't have been telling me their stories.

Many reunions are featured in this book. Antoinette, from Dublin, lost her baby boy in childbirth but met him again at the borders of death. 'I could see two figures beyond the bridge,' she explains.' One was an adult. 'I thought, at the time, that it was my father-in-law who had died just before that. I wasn't sure whether it was him or Our Lord. There was a baby lying on his shoulder. I took it that this was the baby who died. I felt the baby was being minded, being protected.'

Paula, from County Waterford, met her grandfather. 'He was standing in front of the light. His role was to help me over, to be there as a guide,' she says. 'He was just standing there, in profile, at the end of the tunnel. He wasn't saying anything. He was skinny and he looked the way he was when I last knew him, maybe a bit younger. He stood there like a sentry and he didn't look at me. He wasn't connecting with me. But I was very happy to see him. He was a really nice man.'

Usually, around this stage, awe-inspiring encounters with a 'superior being' also take place. Some say that the 'being of light' has no physical features. Instead it radiates power and goodness. It is kind and compassionate. Although those experiencing near-death often can't make out what it looks like, they 'know' it is God. In the sensual world they have entered – without the physical shapes and configurations familiar to us on earth – their remarks make sense.

Sam, who comes originally from Derry, saw the 'superior being' in a cloud which he understood to be heaven. 'I felt that behind this cloud there was some sort of "being,"' he recalls. 'I never saw the being. I couldn't see it. I didn't think it was either male or female. But I felt it was God and I believed I was about to be judged. I felt there was no religion. There was no question about that. It was just one God, as it were.'

Frances, from County Dublin, is similarly unsure of the being's features. 'There was an awful lot of people standing and waiting for me. They were dressed in long white robes,' she remembers. 'There was somebody standing in front of them. He had long hair, with arms outstretched, and was also dressed in a white robe. His arms were outstretched for me.

I didn't recognise that person either. All the time, the bright light was behind him.'

Under the guidance of the 'supreme being', people often undergo a life review. The process frequently involves past-life images flashing before their eyes. In *Going Home* one person I interviewed described the images as resembling a series of 'crystal clear photographs.' Another interviewee described them as 'flashes of events from my life.' This second interviewee said it was 'like flicking through a photo album and experiencing again all the thoughts and emotions I had experienced when the photos were taken.'

The images may be richly coloured and panoramic. Other times they appear in black and white. Hundreds, thousands, perhaps even more of these often three-dimensional views pass by. Normally the scenes are assessed by the person and not by 'God' or anyone else. However, a case history featured in this book differs, with the assessment being conducted by mysterious strangers.

'There were dozens of people on either side and they were all strangers,' Charles, from County Roscommon, reflects. 'They were just looking at me, right through me, like they were judging me. I am positive they were all judging me. I felt they knew everything about me and everything I had done, good and bad. I felt a little bit uncomfortable because of the judging way they looked at me.'

When compiling this book, I also encountered 'forgiveness' as part of the life review – a feature which I have never heard spoken of before. 'It was a "knowing" that I was forgiven,' says Ann, from Dublin, whose review wasn't at first going well. 'It was like mercy being poured over me. It was absolutely blissful. It was the most joyous thing that has ever happened to me.' Since Ann's return, that forgiveness has transformed her life.

Despite these contacts with 'God', most – on restoration to their bodies – become *less* religious in an institutional sense, backing away from established religions. One woman, who was a staunch Catholic, described to me how she is now a 'better Christian' rather than a rigid practitioner of her faith. Helping less-fortunate people has become her vocation in life. Like many others, she professes to be 'spiritual' rather than 'religious'.

It is also notable that fear of dying – so prevalent among the rest of us – tends to disappear following the experience. Death is no longer uncertain or unknown. The prospect of reuniting with loved ones is anticipated with relish. The knowledge that the 'soul', 'spirit', 'mind' or 'consciousness' departs from the body and travels elsewhere, leaving the now-pointless mortal remains behind, is a wonderful comfort. The way ahead is blissful and serene.

Ann, from Connemara, describes her changed views of death: 'I have absolutely no fear or worries about the day when death comes. I feel I will be going towards an ultimate sense of peace. And I wish more people could have that.' Oliver, from County Louth, concurs: 'I wouldn't worry about dying tomorrow, if that's what dying is like. I know that when I die it's going to be something like that. There's nothing to be afraid of. It's going to be very peaceful up there.'

As we know from numerous investigations – and as I have confirmed with my own research – anyone can have a near-death experience, young and old, male and female, and incorporating all cultures, races and creeds. Christians have them. Buddhists and Hindus have them too. Atheists also have them. Even those with no interest in religion have them as well. An estimated one in 20 people say they experience one – although, in truth, probably all of us will have one at the point of death.

Some are referred to as 'hellish' experiences and involve anxious, fearful, sometimes terrifying journeys. A number of unfortunate people find themselves suspended in a state of nothingness, like a vacuum or a void, which they feel they are condemned to endure forever. Others are haunted by guilt or shame pertaining to events from their past lives. More see frightful images of hell, including fire, demons and monsters.

The incidence of these negative experiences is a matter of controversy and debate. Dr. Raymond Moody – the American pioneer of near-death experiences – encountered no 'hellish' case histories in his major 1975 study. Two other prominent researchers – Kenneth Ring and Michael Sabom – found no such experiences either. On the other hand, 'hellish' cases were recorded by the well-known investigators Maurice Rawlings, Margot Grey and Bruce Greyson. Overall, perhaps one in every six, seven or eight experiences is distressing, although the figure may be lower.

My research for this book unearthed only one case. Ann, from Dublin, felt terror. 'I was shown that I wasn't great in life,' she recollects. 'To be more correct, I *knew* I wasn't great in life. I felt that I hadn't been perfectly God-fearing. The feeling was a general one. I hadn't done anything particularly dreadful. But I was human and I knew there were little things I had done that didn't merit whatever goodness was ahead. I had this awful fear and terror of what was going to happen to me.' Fortunately, as you will see later, Ann's story had a happy conclusion.

A further chilling example is the case of British feminist novelist Fay Weldon who, in 2005, went into cardiac arrest following an allergic reaction. She embarked on a very rare 'hellish' trip. There were these pearly gates, she said. 'When they slipped open, there was this terrible creature on the other side. It was trying to pull me through and these other people – presumably the doctors – were trying to pull me back in a tug of war. It wasn't pleasant.' Luckily, the doctors won and Weldon survived.

Other international celebrities have reported better news. My previous book, *Going Home*, described how film stars such as Peter Sellers, Sharon Stone, Elizabeth Taylor and Jane Seymour all witnessed the light. New case histories I have recently uncovered include Larry Hagman, who is best known for his portrayal of J. R. Ewing in *Dallas*. He had a near-death experience following liver-transplant surgery in 1995.

Writing in his autobiography, Hagman described how he 'glimpsed over the edge of this level of existence into the next.' He was welcomed by a figure who he says was neither 'a he nor a she.' The figure informed him that it was not yet time to cross over. He returned to his body a changed man.

In the late 1970s *M*A*S*H* star Donald Sutherland set out on an afterlife journey having contracted meningitis. 'I had gone into a coma and had a near-death experience,' he said. Sutherland floated above his body. The pain, fever and distress suddenly disappeared. Surrounded by a 'soft blue light,' he glided down 'a long tunnel.' He eventually returned to his body and was told by the doctors that he had briefly died.

Around the same time in the late 1970s singer Tony Bennett, following a drug overdose, reached the edge of death where 'a golden light' covered him in 'a warm glow.' The singer – best known for his Grammy Award-winning signature song *I Left My Heart In San Francisco* – sensed he was 'about to embark on a very compelling journey.' He felt peaceful. He was, however, jolted back to life by his wife, who pounded on his chest.

Even the world-renowned psychiatrist, Carl Jung, embarked on a remarkable near-death adventure which he described in his autobiography. 'It seemed to me that I was high up in space,' he wrote. 'Far below I saw the globe of the earth, bathed in a gloriously blue light. I saw the deep blue sea and the continents. Later I discovered how high in space one would have to be to have so extensive a view – approximately a thousand miles!'

Jung was deeply affected by the experience, which took place back in 1944: 'I had the feeling that everything was being sloughed away; everything I aimed at or wished for or thought, the whole phantasmagoria of earthly existence, fell away or was stripped from me – an extremely painful process.' Jung eventually returned to his body and lived for a further 17 years.

As I mentioned earlier, those who undergo near-death experiences frequently report meetings with deceased family and friends who welcome them to the other side. Life-threatening near-death journeys like these, however, are by no means a prerequisite for encountering people who have already crossed over. Instead it is common for dead relatives and friends to return in the form of visions or apparitions.

It is often claimed that the deceased come back to reassure surviving relatives that they are happy and doing well. They also return to help the living in times of danger or need. In addition, it is conjectured that some souls reappear because they are lost on their journeys to the otherworld or are in a transitory stage between lives. All categories have been widely reported in Ireland.

One of the earliest Irish visions dates from the time of St. Malachy in the twelfth century. It is recorded that one night the future saint had a vision of his deceased sister – who was known for her poor sense of morality – standing near the monastery in Lismore, County Waterford where he was living. Remembering that he had neglected to offer mass for her soul for some 30 days, he headed for the church. There he spotted his sister, dressed in a grey robe, outside the door.

Having begun saying mass, he looked again, only to see that the colour of her robe had changed to cream. She had also moved inside the church door but seemed incapable of progressing to the altar. Following further prayer, he saw that her robe had been transformed into a bright white colour and that she was smiling while walking to the top of the church. Malachy's vision became the stuff of legend extending long after his death in 1148, on All Souls' Day, in the course of a journey to Rome.

Eight centuries later, in the 1930s, another example of an Irish vision was reported by the renowned actor and co-founder of Dublin's Gate Theatre, Micheál Mac Liammóir. Writing in his theatrical autobiography *All For Hecuba*, he described the disturbing appearance of his sister Christine. The vision occurred while he was travelling by liner back from the USA, where he had just concluded a tour.

'By my side was my sister Christine, staring at me with sombre eyes,' Mac Liammóir wrote. 'I had not seen her for ten years, but all that day she followed me through the boat, singing and laughing, whispering in my ear, keeping close by my side wherever I went. And by the evening I knew that she was dead.' Shortly after his return to what was then known as Kingsbridge Station (now Heuston Station) in Dublin, Mac Liammóir was informed that his sister had died three days earlier in London.

It is conservatively estimated that one in ten people have seen, heard or felt the presence of someone who wasn't physically there. This was the conclusion reached as far back as 1894 in a major survey undertaken in the UK by the Society For Psychical Research. A much more recent survey from the University of Chicago, published in 1987, found that

42 per cent claimed to have been in contact with a person who was dead. Other studies, in the main, have produced results somewhere in between.

The visions normally reveal themselves in a limited number of ways. Sometimes the deceased present themselves in the exact same physical form they had at the time of death. Other times they appear as if they are younger, fitter or healthier – something which may occur if they have been ravaged by illness or disease at the time they passed away. A number materialise in full profile, from the legs to the top of the head, while more show themselves from the chest upwards.

It is not uncommon for the visions to appear as if in a cloud-like vapour. Sometimes there is no physical shape at all – just a 'sense' or a 'presence' where the witness knows with certainty that they are in the company of someone who has passed on. In other cases there may be familiar smells, strange noises or even sensations of physical contact such as a tap on the shoulder from behind.

Mary, from County Louth, was visited by her young sister who had died in a fire. 'I could see my sister clearly,' Mary recalls. 'She was about the same age as the last time I had seen her, about 12. She was life-sized. But she wasn't in normal clothes and her hair was different. She was wearing like a white, flowing dress and her hair was shorter. I wondered why her hair was shorter because she had lovely long hair when she was alive.'

Phil, from County Cork, felt the presence of her deceased brother while she was being taken to hospital with a heart problem. 'I got in the ambulance and I was lying on the stretcher,' she recollects. 'I was on oxygen and I felt really miserable. I suddenly felt a sort of downwards pressure in the ambulance, as if someone stepped in. I said to the ambulance man, "I'm safe now. My brother is here." I felt my brother's presence. The ambulance man looked around but I said, "You can't see him but I can feel him. He's minding me."'

Another story was told to me by newsreader Anne Doyle. It concerned her brother John who, one day, while out for a walk, saw his deceased mother. 'He came back into the house ashen-faced,' Anne remarks. 'He was as white as a ghost. He said, "I saw Mammy down the field!"' A few weeks later, he collapsed. When asked by Anne how their mother had looked at the time of her appearance her brother said, 'She looked concerned.' Shortly afterwards, he died from cancer.

Mirroring the pattern evident in *Going Home*, many of those interviewed in this book also report that the visions they witness are positioned in the left side of a room. This reflects the observations of esteemed American researcher P. M. H. Atwater who found that the overwhelming majority of cases she encountered were located on the left, particularly in upper left corners.

Confirming Atwater's conclusions, Ethna, in my previous book, was clear about where the vision of her deceased father was situated: 'He appeared in the corner of the bedroom, near a window,' she explained with absolute certainty. 'It was the left-hand corner, as you looked out from the bed. He was up near the ceiling.'

Many observations in this book are similar. Alice, from County Louth, says that her deceased brother also appeared on the left: 'Sometime during the night my brother was there, right beside me, standing against the left bedside locker. I don't know what woke me, whether I sensed him there or not. But I just opened my eyes and there he was.'

Pat Storey, from County Down, describes a visitation from her deceased husband which also appeared on the left: 'I woke up at about eight o'clock. Suddenly Alan was there, over to my left. I could see him as clearly as I can see the table in front of me as I am talking to you now. There was a dressing-table next to the corner of the window and he was between the dressing-table and the window.'

The left again figures in a brace of visions where the deceased is seen to walk across the room. 'In both cases, she passed me from the left to the right,' Wesley, who comes originally from County Monaghan, says of the two visions he had of his deceased wife. 'On the first occasion she came towards me slightly from the left and then disappeared to my right. On the second occasion the door she came from was slightly to the left and she walked straight towards me but again she disappeared to the right.'

In our deliberations so far, we have neglected the sort of fascinating and widely-reported visions which occur when a person is dying. An individual who is fading away will not uncommonly report seeing deceased figures coming to welcome them or to help them cross over. Most, but not all, are former family or friends who are well-known to the person who is expiring. Visions such as these normally occur in the hours or days preceding death.

Many examples of what are commonly referred to as 'death-bed visions' are featured in this book. Among them is a story related by Kathleen Healy, from County Wicklow, concerning the imminent death of her mother. 'Your daddy came to me and he was at the end of the bed!' Kathleen reports her mother as saying. Having pointed to where he had been, her mother then said, 'He smiled at me and I'll be joining him shortly because it's time for me to go. I'll be going home.'

Another interviewee, Marie, from County Waterford, tells of her mother's approaching death: 'Within a week or so before she became very ill she said to me several times, "Daddy has come to me! He was here today!" By that she meant her husband, my father, who had died a long time earlier. Or she would say, "Nan was here!" That's what we used to call her mother, who had also passed away.'

Perhaps the most powerful description ever provided of the death-bed vision came from the pen of the well-respected nineteenth-century Irish author Frances Power Cobbe. Born into Anglo-Irish stock and in later life a friend of Charles Darwin, she wrote a wonderful book in 1882 called *The Peak In Darien*, which espoused her views on personal immortality. It contained a most graphic outline of the death-bed vision.

'The dying person is lying quietly,' Cobbe wrote, 'when suddenly, in the very act of expiring, he looks up – sometimes starts up in bed – and gazes on (what appears to be) vacancy, with an expression of astonishment, sometimes developing instantly into joy, and sometimes cut short in the first emotion of solemn wonder and awe.

'If the dying man were to see some utterly-unexpected but instantly-recognised vision, causing him a great surprise, or rapturous joy, his face could not better reveal the fact. The very instant this phenomenon occurs, death is actually taking place, and the eyes glaze even while they gaze at the unknown sight.'

In 1873, when Cobbe was in her early 50s and at the height of her fame, Ireland welcomed the arrival of William Fletcher Barrett – a Jamaica-born scientist who was appointed Professor of Physics at the Royal College of Science in Dublin. Throughout his distinguished career, Barrett attempted to fuse the scientific principles of physics with the spiritual laws of God. 'Science reveals the garment of God, religion the heart of God,' was how he succinctly articulated his personal philosophy.

Among the case histories recounted by William Barrett in his groundbreaking book *Death-Bed Visions*, which was published in 1926, is a story involving a young girl dying from diphtheria. In the course of telling her mother how to dispose of her few personal belongings, the girl suddenly became alert. Gazing at the ceiling at the far side of the room, and after looking steadily and listening intently for a short time, she said, 'Yes, Grandma, I am coming, only wait just a little while, please.'

Her father asked her, 'Do you see your grandma?' He was aware that her grandmother had died a few years earlier and that the two had been close friends. Surprised at the question, she responded, 'Can't you see her? She is right there waiting for me.' The girl once more turned her attention to the disposal of her few belongings. Having finished, she fixed her eyes on the vision and said, 'Yes, Grandma, I'm coming now.' She then died.

In 1906 Barrett chronicled another case history, this time detailing the death of a young boy aged nine. The boy, we are informed, had recently undergone an operation from which he failed to recover. Despite his condition he was perfectly rational and lucid, fully aware of the presence of his mother, the nurse and the doctor.

Knowing he was dying, the boy held his mother's hands. After a short time he looked up and asked her if she too could see his 'little sister' in the room. 'No, where is she?' his mother asked, aware that his sister had died four years before his birth. 'Right over there. She is looking at me,' he responded.

The boy then exclaimed that he could see a deceased adult acquaintance along with a young friend who had died about a year beforehand. 'I'm going to them,' he said. 'I don't want to leave you, but you'll come to me soon, won't you? Open the door and let them in. They are waiting outside.' Immediately after saying this, he died.

More recently, many well-known international stars have also reported visions or sensations surrounding death. Singer Kylie Minogue, having lost her partner – rock star Michael Hutchence of INXS – to suicide, could still feel his presence after he died. 'Michael's still around, I know that,' she declared. 'He checks in with me. And it's typical of him that I feel his presence just when I need him most or just when something appropriate happens. It's not spooky; it's reassuring, although the force of his presence can be scary.'

Actor Marlon Brando – whose son Christian was convicted of the manslaughter of his half-sister's boyfriend – was convinced that he was being pursued by the dead man. 'I'm being haunted,' Brando said, describing how the spirit of the young man kept whispering 'I should not have died' in his ear. 'It's terrifying,' Brando continued. 'I know it's his angry spirit.'

Fifties' pop music star Tommy Steele described how, while hospitalised with septicaemia as a boy, a small rubber ball repeatedly came bouncing in from the next cubicle. Tommy, who was dying, kept bouncing it back until he got better. Strangely, it transpired that there was no other child, and no ball, anywhere in the ward. He later told his mother what happened.

'What is it, Mum? Tell me,' Tommy asked his mother, whose hands started shaking. She went on to explain that not only had she buried another son Rodney with his favourite rubber ball but she had done so because her cousin had a vision of him playing with the ball on the night he died. 'I came to the conclusion then, and I have never changed my mind, that my brother came to me that night,' the future star of *Half A Sixpence* remarked.

Even the recording of *Free As A Bird* by the three surviving Beatles back in 1995 allegedly took place in the presence of deceased former group member John Lennon whose spirit, according to Paul McCartney, was there. 'There were a lot of strange goings-on in the studio,' McCartney later said, 'noises that shouldn't have been there and equipment doing all manner of weird things. There was just an overall feeling that John was around.'

Another phenomenon often linked to both near-death experiences and visions is the ability to foresee future events. Presuming that the forewarnings are unconnected to either prior information or past experience, they are referred to as 'premonitions' – the word originating from the Latin *prae* meaning 'before' and *monere* meaning 'to warn'. Once again, these gifts or talents – some might even call them 'sensations' – defy explanation.

Premonitions often manifest themselves as vague feelings of unease. A person may be anxious, apprehensive, troubled, distressed and worried that something very bad – such as an accident, disaster or death – is about to occur. Sometimes there is an onset of depression, the cause of which only becomes clear when the disaster takes place. Many report having a 'gut feeling' of troubles ahead.

In this book Kathleen Lawless, from County Wicklow, describes how during New Year's Eve 2008 she unexpectedly plunged into a black depression. 'It was a dreadful black feeling,' she says. 'I had never been like this before.' Her daughter, who lived elsewhere, became unusually 'agitated and uptight' and felt compelled to visit her parents.

Another daughter reported intense feelings of doom when anticipating the year ahead. A son dreamt that he had attended a funeral. To the family's dismay, the husband and father, who was only 66 years of age and medically fit, unexpectedly died of a heart attack the following morning, New Year's Day.

It is also common, once a particular event has unfolded, for people to recall that they had anticipated or 'seen' the event weeks, months or even years in advance. These previews can be uncannily accurate. Some occur during dreams. Others arise while the person is fully lucid and conscious. It is only later, after the event, that their significance becomes readily apparent.

Tony, from County Cavan, recognised something familiar in the scene he witnessed following the death of his father. 'Many years ago, when I was in my late 20s, my father died,' Tony recalls. 'When I went down to his house, they had my father lying on a sofa. When I saw him lying there, it came back to me that about a fortnight previous to that I had seen the exact same vision or dream of my father in that situation. I immediately knew I had been warned about what was going to occur.'

Tony also lost his 21-year-old son, Anthony, in a car crash – a tragic event which was chillingly anticipated in a birthday greeting to the young man just weeks before he died. The sender, a friend from college, drew four stick figures with the largest having a halo over its head and a caption, 'Anthony guiding his friends thro' college.' The friend also wrote, 'I hope sincerely when I go to the pearly gates of heaven to say "hello St. Peter" and of course you will be next to him.' Three weeks later, Anthony was dead.

Another example where an outcome was 'anticipated' was brought to my attention by Colm, from Belfast, whose daughter died from breast cancer in 2006. 'About six weeks before my daughter died, she was down in Dublin getting some radiotherapy,' Colm recollects. 'I wheeled her down from the hospital to a shopping centre and she bought a lot of clothes. I knew she would never wear them. After she picked them out, she realised she had no money with her. It cost me about £1,400 to pay for them on my card.

'Four or five weeks after she died I did the lottery. When I went and checked the ticket I discovered that I had five numbers correct. I didn't have the sixth number, which was 39, the age at which my daughter had died. I had put in 30 instead. At the time I almost felt my hand was guided to do that. If I had put in 39, I would have won £2.5 million. As it was, I won £1,475, which was almost exactly the amount that I had spent on my daughter's clothes. She mustn't have wanted me to win the big amount!'

Perhaps the most famous premonition ever recorded is attributed to President Abraham Lincoln who, shortly before his assassination, saw his forthcoming death in a dream. Speaking to a group of friends at the White House, and in the company of his wife, he described a recent nightmare which was both haunting and disturbing. In it, he saw himself in a 'death-like stillness' while those about him were sobbing and grieving.

Anxious to ascertain the cause of the distress, he dreamt that he walked from room to room in the White House. 'I kept on until I arrived at the East Room,' Lincoln's friend and bodyguard Ward Hill Lamon, who witnessed the conversation, later quoted the President as saying. 'There I met with a sickening surprise. Before me was a catafalque, on which rested a corpse wrapped in funeral vestments.'

Lincoln approached one of the soldiers acting as guards. 'Who is dead in the White House?' he asked. 'The President,' the soldier responded. 'He was killed by an assassin.' Lincoln added: 'Then came a loud burst of grief from the crowd, which woke me from my dream.' Abraham Lincoln was shot by John Wilkes Booth three days later, on 14 April 1865. He died the following morning.

Additional premonitions are associated with the *Titanic's* maiden voyage, which came to a disastrous conclusion on the night of 14 – 15 April 1912. At least 55 people changed their minds about sailing on the ship at short notice. The list included John Pierpont Morgan, who was ultimate owner of the White Star Line, and his former business partner Robert Bacon, who was the departing American Ambassador to France. Others included the steel magnate Henry C. Frick and the railway and shipping mogul George W. Vanderbilt.

Among those lost in the disaster was Chief Officer Henry Wilde, who had reluctantly joined the crew. In a letter posted during the ship's stopover at Cobh, he wrote to his sister: 'I still don't like this ship ... I have a queer feeling about it.' Despite his reservations, Wilde sailed to his death on the liner. One of the ship's firemen John Coffey, from Cobh, was luckier – he hid himself in one of the postbags and smuggled himself ashore before the liner set sail following its brief stopover in County Cork.

Undoubtedly the most puzzling *Titanic* premonition – or strange coincidence, if it should be such – involved the novel *Futility* which was published 14 years before the ship sank. Written by the American amateur mystic Morgan Robertson, the similarity between the contents of his book and the actual details pertaining to the *Titanic* were startling.

Robertson's fictional ship, ominously called the *Titan*, had virtually the same top speed, capacity, length, number of lifeboats, number of passengers, number of propellers and displacement as the *Titanic*. The two ships sailed under the British flag. Both sailed in April – and both hit an iceberg and sank.

Premonitions were likewise reported prior to the disaster which took place in the Welsh mining village of Aberfan back in 1966. On Friday 21 October, 116 children and 28 adults died when a river of coal waste and boulders slid down from a man-made mountain and crashed into a school. Most of the schoolchildren who died were aged between seven and ten.

Although many claimed *following* the event to have had forebodings of the disaster, one story *predated* the tragedy and had the ring of cast-iron truth. The story concerned ten-year-old Eryl Mai Jones who earlier that week had said to her mother, 'I'm not afraid to die. I shall be with Peter and June.'

The day before the catastrophe she also spoke of a dream. 'I dreamt I went to school and there was no school there,' she said. 'Something black had come down all over it.' Eryl Mai Jones died on that unfortunate day in 1966 and was later buried alongside her friends Peter and June.

Before concluding this chapter it is worth considering the overall significance of the phenomena examined above – premonitions, visions and near-death experiences. Between them, they account for some of the most mysterious and puzzling yet commonplace occurrences known to mankind. Perplexingly, most of them elude, by miles, any sort of scientific explanation.

By any standards, they are prolific. An estimated 300,000 Irish people, north and south of the border, will report a near-death experience. A larger number – a minimum of 600,000 – will have seen or sensed an apparition or vision. A much higher figure again – up to one-quarter of the population – will have some sort of premonition. Even if we haven't experienced one for ourselves, we all know of someone who has.

Why some people experience them while others experience nothing at all is something of a mystery. On reflection, however, it may not be quite so strange. Perhaps many of us, although capable of experiencing supernatural sensations and happenings, resist them, deny them or disguise them. Maybe only some of us embrace them, absorb them or even recognise that they have taken place.

Certain factors may have a crucial role to play. A tolerant upbringing, where similar issues are openly discussed and welcomed, may be significant. A sensitive nature, compassion for other people, a belief in the unity of all life forms, being comfortable with disorder and being open to the prospects of an afterlife may also be relevant.

Either way, the experiences have profound significance for our understanding of life after death. For most of us, death is taboo. We obsess about it but seldom speak of it. We sanitise it and banish it from our eyes. We live out our lives as if it will never take place. We run from it, yet hope that it won't mark the end of the story. We pray for a happy one, yet hope it never occurs.

What you are about to read will help to redress this ambivalence about death. Those who are featured in the chapters ahead provide insights to a very different world, a different dimension, a place of the senses where something exists that transcends earthly time and space. It is the otherworld, the afterlife, the ultimate destination where our 'consciousness', 'mind', 'soul' or 'spirit' is said to survive after the body shuts down. The following Irish stories describe this, the last and greatest frontier.

NEAR-DEATH JOURNEYS

The eminent American researcher and cardiologist Dr. Michael Sabom was heckled at the conclusion of one of his lectures. The fact that he raised some people's ire was not in itself remarkable. He was, after all, speaking on a topic – the near-death experience – that often generated heated debate. Much more surprising, however, was that the interruption came from a fellow cardiologist who was seated in the audience.

Obviously unimpressed by Dr. Sabom's presentation, the furious medic declared that in his 30 years in practice he had brought numerous people back from the edge of death. 'I've been in the middle of this stuff for years,' he protested. 'And I've never talked to a patient who had one of these near-death experiences.' Before Sabom could reply, another man in the audience stood up and exclaimed, 'I'm one of the people you saved and I'll tell you right now, you're the last person I would ever tell about my near-death experience.'

That story, related by another notable researcher Dr. Raymond Moody in his bestseller *The Light Beyond*, helps explain why the near-death experience has remained hidden and concealed, some might even say covered up, over the centuries. The medical profession, to put it mildly, were unsympathetic. 'They are dreams,' doctors said. 'They are hallucinations. They are pharmaceutically induced. Don't be silly. Ignore them. Forget them,' they advised.

Few people, as a result, were brave enough to own up. They risked ridicule if they did so. Those who spoke out were dismissed as being odd, strange or even deranged. Most, it was said, were religious fanatics. Almost all did the wise thing – they kept quiet. Out of sight, out of mind, the near-death phenomenon was secreted away within families or more likely stored in the dark recesses of individual minds.

The publication of Dr. Raymond Moody's seminal book *Life After Life* back in 1975 changed all that. It had a seismic impact. An age-old phenomenon was instantly given definition, substance and meaning. A range of components was identified – departure from the body, tunnel travel, feelings of peace, seeing the light, meetings with family or friends, encounters with a 'superior being', life reviews, decisions to stay or come back and lives which are transformed upon return, among others. Moody christened the phenomenon the 'near-death experience'.

The cat was out of the bag. Leaving our bodies was a much more peaceful process than we had previously believed. Kathleen Hammond, from County Dublin, articulated the feeling more than four decades after her experience occurred. 'The peace was wonderful,' she told me. 'I felt so calm, so tranquil and so serene. I didn't feel I had a body, only that I was some sort of being. There was no pain, no worry and no fear. It was like I was in another dimension. I think I was heading for the beyond.'

Many others stepped forward to tell their stories. Not everyone shared every element of the experience or, if they did, they certainly couldn't remember them all. Not everyone experienced the elements in the same sequence. Not all of the experiences were particularly good. Above all, although the basic fundamentals were commonly shared, the specific details differed. The stories they told me, however, were unquestionably sincere. You can gauge that for yourself from what follows.

PAULA, FROM COUNTY WATERFORD, had a classic near-death experience in the summer of 1985.

I got very sick during June and July of 1985. I was 30 at the time and was working very hard. I developed an autoimmune disease although I didn't realise it and the doctors didn't realise it either. My skin became discoloured. Internally my lungs and my kidneys were being attacked by my immune system. I was very sick.

During the June bank holiday weekend I couldn't breathe. I was coughing up blood and had aches and pains. I collapsed and had to go into hospital. I was in there for two weeks and was half-conscious at that stage. The doctors didn't know what it was. So they sent me home.

I collapsed again and was taken by ambulance back into hospital. I don't remember much of what happened after that. My kidneys were being attacked and my lungs, in particular, were being attacked. I wasn't able to breathe and I was on oxygen. I had a huge temperature. It was all very stressful. But they eventually figured out what it was. One doctor told my husband, 'She is either going to die or she will have permanent kidney failure.'

At some stage I had this experience, like I was moving away from the real world. I was in a large dark tunnel. It was dark brown rather than black. I didn't walk through the tunnel – instead I floated through it. I was just moving at the pace that it took to understand what was happening. I wasn't worried. I felt hugely at peace. The feeling was lovely. I felt I was going on a journey, like I was going home.

In front of me was this crystal-white light. The light was

the goal. It was the place to go to. It wasn't dazzling. It was really bright and deep, like a good-quality crystal. I knew it was the next stage and I knew that behind it was an awful lot more. I didn't think it was heaven but I knew it was life afterwards. I also knew that what was beyond it was a huge, benign, extremely-caring presence. It was God.

I could clearly see my grandfather, who had died nine years before, at the end of the tunnel. He was standing in front of the light. His role was to help me over, to be there as a guide. He had been with me for a while during my sickness. In fact, sometime beforehand, back in April or May, at a time when I was beginning to get sick, I had found myself to be very much in his presence. He was constantly around me and in my thoughts. His presence, at that time, was very real.

Now he was just standing there, in profile, at the end of the tunnel. He wasn't saying anything. He was skinny and he looked the way he was when I last knew him, maybe a bit younger. He stood there like a sentry and he didn't look at me. He wasn't connecting with me. But I was very happy to see him. He was a really nice man. I had loved him madly. Around him were lots of other people or 'spirits' or what I would call 'others' who were going to help me as well.

All the time I was digesting things. I felt things were being explained. As I went further on, I felt I knew more. I had 'knowledge' of things. There came a stage where I felt I was going to leave my children behind. I had two small children and I thought, 'My time has gone and it's their life now.' I was going to leave them. I felt it was natural. I was very accepting even though if I thought that now, I know I would be in tears.

As I got further on I knew I wasn't going to die. I was sure of it. I could see a definite black-and-white cut-off between the end of the tunnel and the light. I wasn't allowed to go near that edge. I then heard a voice saying, 'It's not your time!

You have a job to do! You have to go back!' The voice didn't belong to any particular person. It was neutral, kind and warm. They were the specific words that were used. And I knew that the job was to look after my two children.

Suddenly I was back in my body. I was in and out of consciousness for a while. They put me on a severe treatment. I was still very sick and in hospital for seven weeks. It took me a long time to recover. But, when I came around, I knew I had been somewhere. I knew something big had happened. Everything was different.

What happened changed my life in huge ways. I now believe we are meant to do something meaningful with our lives. And I now have knowledge of what is there after death. When they say 'God cares about everything', I know that it's true. I have confirmed it. I know I was in God's presence. And I know that this being has huge caring and kindness. I understand the huge compassion that is there.

I also know that religions don't matter because what happened to me is going to happen to everybody, anyway. There's no point in believing in one religion or another religion. And it is meaningless to get strung up about it being a big sin to not go to mass on a Sunday. It became crystal clear to me that there's a huge difference between being religious and being spiritual.

I wouldn't mind going on the journey again. I don't fear it. The bit I fear is what happens before it, like dying in a car crash or whatever. I would like to have time with my family to tell them I am dying. I would say to them, 'I'm sad but I'll see you again.' But I know where I will be going. It's as clear now as it was then. And the meaning of it stays as deep as ever. It really does stay with you, having seen the other side.

ANTOINETTE MURRAY, FROM DUBLIN, also had a classic experience – this time back in 1971.

I lost a baby boy back in 1971. I was very weak after the birth. They let me go home from the maternity hospital and, as far as I know, there was some afterbirth left inside me. I haemorrhaged twice. By the time they got me back into hospital, about ten days later, I was very ill and losing blood all the time. I haemorrhaged again back in the hospital. I nearly died and they had to give me pints and pints of blood.

I was lying in my hospital bed when, suddenly, I could literally feel the life going out of me. I went down this bright tunnel of light. There was beautiful light all around. There was no blackness. It wasn't like a black tunnel. It also wasn't a case of light here and there. It was just full of white, bright light.

I was floating down the tunnel. It was like I was on a bed, face forward. I was there for a while. I wanted to keep going and I wanted to get to the end of the tunnel. There was a door at the end, which was half-open. The door was light coloured as well.

Beyond the door was a garden. It was absolutely beautiful. Everything was very lush and coloured green. It was also full of lovely, coloured flowers. The flowers had colours like red and yellow. It was a place you would want to go to, a place you would want to be in.

There was a bridge in the garden, which you could go up on and walk over. It was a lovely Japanese type of bridge. There were bars along the side of the bridge and there was a trickle of water under it. The water was like a little river going through the flowers.

I could see two figures beyond the bridge. One was an adult who was dressed in a white robe. He had long hair.

I thought, at the time, that it was my father-in-law who had died just before that. I wasn't sure whether it was him or Our Lord. There was a baby lying on his shoulder. The baby was lying into him. I took it that this was the baby who died. I felt the baby was being minded, being protected.

The big thing I remember was trying to get through the door. I wondered, 'Will I make it there?' All I wanted to do was just get into the garden. It wasn't particularly that I wanted to get to the two figures. I just wanted to get to this place. I desperately wanted to be there.

As I got to the door I regained consciousness. I was so disappointed to be back. The sense of disappointment was awful. It was terrible to wake up and say, 'God! I'm back here!' I just wanted to be asleep and go down there again and get into the garden.

I believe I was dying that night and I was on a journey and something brought me back. I would say it to my friends and people like that. And sometimes I'd hear something about it on the radio and say, 'That happened to me.' But that's as far as it went.

Looking back, I know I was brought back for a reason. I had a young baby girl at home and I had my husband. I don't know whether it was that I chose to come back for them, that I felt there was still work for me to do here. But I definitely feel now, at this stage of my life, that I was meant to come back that night. I know it wasn't my time to go.

When I got over the trauma, and all the rest of it, I was left without a fear of dying. I felt, 'If I can get to that place, and if it's going to be like that, it's going to be lovely, it's going to be rosy.' I also know that I will meet up with my baby again. I have no doubt about that. So the prospect of dying hasn't worried me since.

CHARLES LAVIN, FROM COUNTY ROSCOMMON, encountered strangers who judged him during a near-death experience he had in 1965.

I was born with a major heart defect. I had a badly burst left ventricle. It was burst from top to bottom. There was a hole into it. In 1963 they gave me three years to live. Then, in 1965, a specialist agreed to operate on me in London. I was 25 at the time. It was going to be a very big operation, where they would open up my chest and take out the heart.

They were going to close the hole up with metal clips and they needed 15 metal clips to do it. They were going to do a graft as well. The operation was scheduled for 5 November 1965. So I went into hospital and the operation went ahead as planned.

They began the operation and, even though I was under anaesthetic, the next thing was that I could feel a sharp pain in the middle of the chest. It only lasted about a third of a second. Suddenly I left my body and floated up to the ceiling. I don't know how high the ceiling was but I felt I was quite high. The doctors and nurses and complicated machinery seemed quite small.

I could see everybody below me. There were six people there and three nurses. They were all in their greenish outfits, with hats. They were all fussing around. There was a semi-panic going on. I could see my own body on the bed, with my own face. I knew it was me and I knew I was dead. I was positive of that. But, although I could see everything, I couldn't make out the part of my body where they were operating because they were over it and there were cloths or towels over it as well.

I felt very warm, cosy and peaceful. I couldn't describe the feeling of peace, it was so profound. There was no pain. I had no fear, none whatsoever. I shouted down, at the top of the lungs, telling them that it was alright and that I was dead. I knew my body was dead and I didn't mind but they didn't hear me. I must have shouted twice but they never responded. They just kept working away.

Then I went flying through a big black tunnel. It was very dark and it was very broad, about maybe eight or ten feet in diameter. I went through it very fast. I could hear a 'whoosh' in my ear, a rushing sound like wind. I was going at an awful rate, really flying. I was face forward but I thought my head was a bit higher than my feet. Yet I think I was travelling in a horizontal direction.

Next thing I went through a big bright light. It was a big broad light, the width of the tunnel. It wasn't blinding or dazzling at all. I could see it approaching before I went through it. I flashed through it. I was only a split second in it when, suddenly, I went into slow motion and everything changed.

I was moving along a narrow path and there were rows of people on each side of me. It looked like there was a mist in the path between the two rows of people. As I put my foot down into the mist, my foot would disappear. I couldn't see my foot although I could see my knee coming up out of the mist again. When my foot went down it became invisible but when it came up I could see it again. It was like I was trotting in slow motion.

There were dozens of people on either side and they were all strangers to me. The people looked very ordinary, each one dressed in different attire, like you would meet in town. I couldn't make out their faces although there was one face that seemed familiar. But, for the rest of them, I would just see their faces very quickly and then they were gone.

They were just looking at me, right through me, like they

were judging me. I am positive they were all judging me. I felt they knew everything about me and everything I had done, good and bad. I felt a little bit uncomfortable because of the judging way they looked at me. It was like I was going between them and trying to look ahead even though I knew they were there.

I suddenly started looking forward to meeting up with my grandfather and grandmother who were dead, and my father who had died of a brain haemorrhage in 1946 and my mother who had died in 1960, but they weren't there. The only people who were there were strangers.

Eventually I got so far down between the rows of people and they all started looking at each other and shaking their heads. It was like they were saying, 'He's not going to be allowed to stay!' I felt a great sense of loss or disappointment. I had the feeling I was going to have to go back and that's exactly what I did.

Before I came back I turned around and looked at them all. I remember I turned to the right and, as I started going back for the light, I looked over my shoulder and I saw a tall being on my left-hand side. He was looking after me. He was like a monk, very clean, wearing a bright-grey or an off-white cowl. The cowl had a belt which was loose. I said, 'That must be Christ!' I looked for the face but there was no face, just blackness. He was looking after me as I went away from him.

Then I flew right through the light. It was really fast, instantaneous. I didn't notice the tunnel coming back, just the light. The next thing I was on a trolley, being wheeled down the corridor. I opened my eyes and looked up at the man who was pushing me. He said, 'It's alright, Mr. Lavin, your operation is over.' The whole thing probably took only about three-quarters of a minute. Time had taken on a different dimension.

Looking back, I am certain about what happened and I know it was real. I feel I went to a different world. I feel I died and was on the borders of the next life. I am positive about that. I couldn't say it was heaven but it was a very happy experience. I was very contented and comforted. I wanted to stay there. And I now have no fear about dying. I look forward to going again.

I rarely go to mass or confession. I used to but I got out of it and a couple of years after the operation I stopped going to church. I don't think it matters. But it does matter to be a good person. That's what I think is important. When people talk about death, that's when I think about it. And I tell them if they have a good life there's nothing to fear.

ANN HESLIN, FROM DUBLIN, **had a most extraordinary experience immediately after the birth of her daughter. The journey she went on changed her life.**

In 1986 I was pregnant with my third child. They took me in early to have her because I'd had a previous Caesarean section. I had a section again. They put me under anaesthetic and I was terrified. I could hear them talking and I was so sure I was going to feel the cut and everything else. It was like I was trapped. I felt terrorised. Then I heard Áine screaming and she was delivered a fine, healthy baby girl.

As soon as I heard her screaming I travelled through this tunnel of bright lights and I was going at a great speed. It happened very suddenly. The tunnel was completely filled with single lights. There was no blackness at all. Everything was well lit. There were lights everywhere. It wasn't like a single light. Instead there were flashes of light, like they were sparkling.

I was going along the tunnel at great speed. The tunnel

surrounded me closely so it wasn't that big. I wasn't walking. I was just travelling through it. I was going straight forward, not up or down. I can't say if it was my face that was forward because I can't even say if my body was there. I can't recall being in my body. It was more like a consciousness going through.

I saw these mysteries regarding faith. They were just like insights or revelations. I don't know what they were but I definitely think they were related to our faith. Whether they were about 'three persons in the one God' or whatever, I don't know. I can never recall what they were, to my regret. But I associated them with religion.

They were coming up in front of me. I was amazed by them. They seemed very simple. I was saying, 'Oh, my God! If only we'd known!' There might have been ten of them but I'm not sure. That's only a rough guess because they were so quick and I was so gobsmacked. As each was shown I knew what it was but then it was gone. My big regret was that I wouldn't be able to share them and I felt I had no proof.

I also felt terror. I was shown that I wasn't great in life. To be more correct, I *knew* I wasn't great in life. I felt that I hadn't been perfectly God-fearing. The feeling was a general one. I hadn't done anything particularly dreadful. But I was human and I knew there were little things I had done that didn't merit whatever goodness was ahead. I had this awful fear and terror of what was going to happen to me.

I'm sure part of it was because of guilt over my mother. I had prayed and cried in despair, for four years, because of my relationship with her. I adored her. But, after my father died, my mother moved in with us. I was very close to her and my husband was very fond of her. She was more than welcome but it wasn't a healthy thing to happen. She took over my life. I was her child again. She always said, 'Two women in the kitchen never get on.'

I was lucky that I worked because I knew that if we had been at home together it would have been hard on both of us. I'd come home and I'd try to be different but after five minutes I'd be pulling my hair out. That went on for four years. It was a dreadful place to be. It just didn't work and I nearly went out of my mind.

My problem was guilt and I couldn't understand anyone being like this – resenting a mother's presence. I felt like an Antichrist. I was ashamed of my feelings. That's possibly what was on my mind in the tunnel. I suppose I thought I was going to hell. Hell didn't come into it at the time but that's how I interpreted it later. It was a terrorising feeling. I was really convinced that I wouldn't have a second chance. It was very uncomfortable.

Then I was shown what I felt were words but I don't remember a voice. It was probably more like a feeling. It was a 'knowing' that I was forgiven. It was like mercy being poured over me. All was forgiven and I knew it was. I felt, 'After the life I have led, I'm forgiven and I'm going to heaven!'

It was absolutely blissful. It was the most joyous thing that has ever happened to me. It was absolutely wonderful. I would have stayed there if I could. I didn't think, 'I have three children and a husband that I have to go back to.' That didn't come into it. It was just that I was there and I was going to heaven.

Suddenly I felt I was going backwards, away from heaven. I was still looking back at it although I can't say what I was seeing. Then I came back and I might have said out loud, 'There's my place in heaven!' I feel I might have said that but

I don't know. I just knew a place in heaven was being kept for me.

I didn't meet anybody during this journey. I saw nobody and I don't remember a voice. What I heard was an inner voice, if you like. But that wasn't really a voice – it was more like inner thoughts. The only people I met were two nurses when I came back. I seemed to be still looking back at my place in heaven when I saw them.

One of them was an elderly sister who was a kindly old soul. She was standing over me with another nurse. She was telling me about the baby and how she had lived against all the odds. She said, 'She's here for a reason.' I knew the reason. I knew she had brought me to heaven and it was meant to be.

I often wondered how I appeared to the nurses after I came back. The same sister would often come around to my bed afterwards. I was in for ten days after the section. She would sit on the chair beside my bed and chat to me. The doctor who delivered the baby came around too. I often wondered if they were trying to give me an opportunity to say something or give them an opportunity to ask. But I didn't. And I'm sorry now that I didn't.

It was a life-changing experience and I'm so much the better for it. I got great peace when I came back. I was kind of hugging myself. I probably sickened people because I couldn't stop saying, 'Oh! I feel so wonderful!' I was physically well. I was mentally at peace and I loved everybody. I can say my heart was opened and it was said to me that it was my miracle.

I also had loved my mother but I needed to grow up and become independent. She had already gone from the house since my second child was born. I couldn't talk to her or explain how I felt. I couldn't hurt her. But my husband talked to her and to this day I don't know what he said. But she went home. She had her own home and she visited occasionally. She also came to visit when I had my third baby. There was no awkwardness. Instead there was this warmth. Everybody noticed. I was so, so at peace.

The bliss remained for a couple of years afterwards. The feeling lived on. I feel that if it had been a dream it couldn't have had that effect. Even afterwards, when I'd think about death, I would get this little thrill in the heart. I didn't want to die but I was probably looking forward to that experience again. It certainly helped me with my fear of death.

I have no doubt about what happened. I would be a bit reluctant to tell certain people because I know they'd just laugh. But I'd tell my good friends – people I've got to know very well – and I feel they understand.

I also believe I'm going to heaven unless I do something dreadful and I don't intend to. I try to stay close to God but it's not always possible. I go to mass every Sunday. That's all. I don't go more often. But I'm a better person. I became very unselfish, I think. I also feel it's there for everybody, if we knew how to get it.

ANN HENNING JOCELYN, WHO LIVES IN CONNEMARA **but who comes originally from Sweden, had her experience in 1967. It occurred in Gothenburg, Sweden, where she was living at the time.**

I was 19 years old and I was working for a car hire firm as a stopgap before going to college. One day I was sent out to collect a car that had been left at the airport. When I went out I realised there was a very bad snowstorm, with freezing fog and snow on top of ice. The conditions were bad.

I got into the car, which was a small saloon car like a Ford Fiesta or something like that. I began driving back on the dual carriageway. Suddenly the wheels lost their grip and I lost contact with the road. I saw a large concrete post coming towards me. It was by the side of the road and it was very thick. It might have held a street light or something. I saw it coming closer and closer. I was out of control and I hit it head-on.

The post went straight through the middle of the car. It cut into the car to about as far as the back seat. It sliced past me. The gearbox was found 200 metres away. I got the steering-wheel into my body. I blacked out and I woke up hearing voices with someone shouting, 'We must get her out before it explodes!'

I was pulled out and was lying on the cold, snowy ground. I was taken into hospital. I was brought into A&E and I was lying on a trolley. I heard these terrible noises, like someone in pain and groaning. It sounded quite eerie. I looked around to see who it was and when I opened my eyes I saw everyone else in the A&E staring with great concern at me because it was *me*. I was the one who was groaning.

Eventually I was admitted. They looked at me and said, 'There doesn't seem to be much wrong with you.' Then they realised that my ankle was broken. They said, 'You're very lucky. There isn't anything else wrong with you but we will wait until the morning to put you in plaster and the surgeon will look at you then.'

The following morning, when I was coming to, I saw a man looking at me. It was the surgeon in his scrubs. He said, 'Can you see me?' I just about could. He said, 'We have been giving you oxygen to help wake you up because we can't anaesthetise you unless you're conscious.' He realised I was deeply unconscious. So they X-rayed me but they couldn't see anything on the X-ray.

The reason why they couldn't see anything on the X-ray

was because I was so full of blood. I was dying of internal bleeding. I was in critical condition. They rang my mother to say I was critical and they were going to operate to save my life. They said, 'We can't promise anything because we don't know where the bleeding is coming from.'

They were hoping it was the spleen because, if it was, they could have just lifted it out and drained the abdomen. But they found out it was my liver and, at that time, a ruptured liver could not be repaired. The young surgeon had been taught that if you find a patient in my condition all you can do is let them die.

However, the surgeon said, 'She's 19 years old. I can't let her die. I'm going to try a new method.' The method involved using thread that can be absorbed by the body. This thread had just been invented. It had never been used in the hospital before. He said, 'I'm going to have a go!' So he did. He sewed up my liver and I survived.

Towards the end of the operation I found myself in this tunnel. The tunnel was like a dark void. It surrounded me. If I was to describe it, it would have been about six feet wide and about the same height. The walls were just darkness. I was passing through it, walking. I was moving quite freely, at a comfortable pace.

At the end of the tunnel was this light. It was about 50 yards away. It wasn't a sharp light, just shimmering and appealing. It was more yellow in colour, like sunshine. It was like a space that was lit by the sun. It was a little bit like if you were walking in a forest and you saw a glade, you'd want to go to it. It's like an instinctive thing – you'd want to come out of the darkness. I just wanted to go to the light.

I was all alone. I had no fear although I didn't know where I was going. There was no discomfort. I felt calm and at peace. I just felt there was something good waiting for me where I was going. It was definitely somewhere peaceful and comforting. It was like I was going home.

I hesitated for a moment and I tried to think of things that could hold me back, like my dog and my boyfriend and my mother – my father was dead. I thought of them all but I realised that they didn't really matter to me. They were already so far away. I didn't feel any sadness. It was much more attractive to go towards this light.

Suddenly, as I was approaching the light, I was torn back. There were three nurses there, pulling at me and begging me not to go to sleep. I can remember their faces to this day and I remember the tears in their eyes. They were crying because they knew that if I didn't wake up, that was the end. They knew what was happening to me. They knew that if I lost consciousness I wouldn't come back.

All I wanted was to continue towards this light. I just wanted to be on my way. I really wanted to sleep and I had no interest in anything on earth. There was absolutely nothing to hold me back. There was such a comfort in that thought. But I came back for the nurses' sake because they had worked so hard and they cared so deeply. I really didn't feel I could let them down. They looked relieved although I felt resigned because I knew what I had left behind.

Just to show how far gone I was, my mother, who had been going through a terrible time not knowing whether I was going to live or not and had been waiting in the hospital, was finally allowed to come in and see me. I looked at her and I said, 'Oh! Are you here? What are you doing here?' She said, 'I've come to see you.' I said, 'Why is that?' She was totally taken aback and said, 'But don't you understand? I've been sitting here all this time waiting to see how you were doing.'

I said, 'Really? Why didn't you go to work?' She said, 'I couldn't work while you were still ill.' I said, 'Really? Did you care that much?' I had been so removed from my own relationships that I found it very hard to believe that I meant so much to her because she meant so little to me at the time. She was terribly taken aback. But I know exactly why I said that and how I felt because my personal relationships had ceased to matter.

Afterwards I always knew I had experienced death. It's in the face of death that we become in touch with ourselves. I think we can learn a lot from our encounters, whether it is the deaths of people close to us or our own near-death. It may sound strange but I think there's a beauty in the closeness of death because it puts everything in perspective. It did that for me and it does that for others too.

I don't mind the thought of dying. In fact, I never feel sad for people who are dying, only for those left behind. I also sometimes feel the longing to return to where I once had been. That is not necessarily a good thing. It is still something I occasionally have to battle against when life becomes difficult. It's something I have to distance myself from. But it's there. And I have absolutely no fear or worries about the day when death comes. I feel I will be going towards an ultimate sense of peace. And I wish more people could have that.

SAM, WHO COMES FROM DERRY but who lives in the UK, had two near-death experiences, one in 2005 and the other in 2006. They resulted from problems with blocked arteries.

I was a very competitive athlete when I was young, right from my teens. I ran for a club in Derry and was always very fit. I used to compete in events. I ran for my school and also played football at school. With the exception of a short time in the early 1960s, I kept it going all my life. I always had a tracksuit.

When I was 65 I was living in Bromley, Kent. There was a park nearby. It's a lovely park. I used to run maybe four times a week, for about five miles. One day I was running there, on my own, and I started feeling unwell. I came to a slight incline in the park. I thought, 'I feel terribly rough.' I felt extremely tired. It felt as if I needed to sit down. But I ran through it.

When I reached the top I felt this awful pain in my chest. It was like somebody hit me with a baseball bat. It was like a real thump. I was conscious for a little while, enough to know that something serious had happened to me. The thought went through my mind, 'This is a stroke!' even though to this day I don't know what a stroke is. As it turned out, I was actually having some sort of heart attack.

I looked around to see if I could see anybody or if anybody could see me. I could see a golfer in a nearby golf course but he was just going on his merry way. I couldn't speak anyway because I had no more strength. I remember I put my hand back to my hip-pocket to see if I had any identity on me. It's marvellous what you do! I then lost consciousness.

I fell down on the ground. The doctor told me later that that's what more or less saved my life. He told me that blocked arteries had caused what happened, the same thing my grandmother had died of. But because I had fallen down, and my pulse rate lowered while I was unconscious, just enough blood got through to bring me back to life without killing me. The higher pulse rate would have killed me.

Either way, no blood was getting through my heart at the time I collapsed. In those few minutes I was either dead or whatever. When the blood started to flow through again I came back to life. People have often asked me, 'How long were you in that state of collapse, in the park?' The answer is, 'I don't know.' It probably was for five minutes or something like that.

Suddenly I was gone from my body and I was in this very bare place. It was like being on the top of this massive dome which was as big as the earth. It was slightly curved, as if it was the world. It wasn't coloured. There was no green or anything else. Everything was dark, a greyish mud colour. It felt like being in the middle of nowhere. There was nobody there.

I never felt such peace in all my life. It was unbelievable. It was a sublime sense of peace. Everything was tranquil. I started to think about the earth and about trials and tribulations in life. I could see things in a different perspective. Everybody was flying around the world like ants. It was a different time zone. I realised that the world only lasted a very short period of time. I also realised that people come and go and they make mistakes.

In the distance was a cloud. It was white, on a dark-grey background. It was bright but it didn't blind me. It was like what they call a cumulus cloud, puffy and circular. Either the cloud was rolling towards me or I was going towards it. I couldn't really tell. I'm not certain. Either way, I felt that it was heaven.

I felt that behind this cloud there was some sort of 'being'. I never saw the being. I couldn't see it. I didn't think it was either male or female. But I felt it was God and I believed I was about to be judged. I felt there was no religion. There was no question about that. It was just one God, as it were.

There was a sort of 'swirling' around the edges of this cloud and it seemed that figures were starting to develop. They seemed to be in human form and were just at the periphery of the cloud. It seemed to me that they were outriders, in celestial form, for the being behind the cloud. It seemed they were escorting the being along. But they never quite got to fruition.

Suddenly I heard from behind the cloud, 'You've been OK! Do you want to stay here? If you want to stay here, you can! But if you have any unfinished business to do, you may go back!' I felt, 'I don't want to stay here because of my grand-children.'

Just as I said that, I felt like I had moved back slightly. I was still looking at the same place and the same scene. The cloud was still there but I was back from it. It now looked like I was looking at a sort of television screen which included the cloud. At the bottom of that screen I could see my four grandchildren. They were off the edge of the screen, to my left. They came to the edge of the screen and just disappeared.

Then I woke up in the park. I looked around. I didn't feel as much pain as before. The blood was starting to flow again. My pulse rate had lowered. I was still on my own. I picked myself up and wondered, 'Gosh! What was that? What has happened?' I made my way to where I normally had a rest after I did my run. There were seats there. I then went back down to my car and drove home.

I went to the doctors. They did a test on me by putting a tube up through my arteries into my heart. They told me I had blocked arteries and I had to get the problem fixed. They didn't know if I would need a bypass or if they would be able to put a stent in. But I was lucky that the area that was causing the problem was in a straight line and they could put in a stent.

I had the operation on 10 January 2006. I was warned beforehand that I was going to get a pain in my chest when they did the procedure. They said I was going to feel the same as I did that day in the park. They told me to be prepared for it. But they told me it wouldn't last long, just a short while. Then it would all be finished and I would be fine.

Exactly as they said, I started to feel the pain in my chest when they did the procedure. Unfortunately it didn't stop. The pain became very severe. The doctor who was doing it had his back to me. I couldn't even roll off the table to indicate to him what was going on. I then started to lose consciousness and I could vaguely see the odd white coat around me.

Suddenly I was in exactly the same place as I had been three months earlier. The dome-like surface was there. The cloud was there. I felt that extraordinary sense of peace. I heard the voice again. There were the figures coming on the periphery of the cloud.

Again I was told, 'You haven't been bad! You have done OK! You can stay here or, if you have any unfinished business, you may go!' It was like being told, 'You can stay here and witness bliss all the time or you can go back to where you came from.'

Then I moved away again and saw the whole scene as if within a screen. My grandchildren were there again, at the edge. It was all exactly the same. Then I woke up. The doctors had seen I was under stress and had injected something into me. I had become an emergency case. I could see there was a lot going on around me when I woke up. Then everything subsided and I was back to life.

Afterwards I couldn't believe what had happened to me. I thought about it a lot and still do. I thought, 'That was a strange experience!' I thought, 'Nobody will ever believe me when I tell them about it.' I told some people and a few disregarded what I described and said, 'You were only dreaming.' But it wasn't like that at all.

What happened has changed my view about religion. The experience had nothing to do with religion at all. It was about one 'supreme being'. Who we are going to meet isn't going to be a Muslim or a Catholic or whatever. After it happened to me I was speaking to a colleague of mine who was a Muslim. I remember telling him about this being and the feeling of peace. I told him that there was just one God and that religion didn't matter. He thought that was most important. He was very surprised by it.

What also came across was that you didn't have to be perfect in life. That was clear when I was told, 'You haven't done too bad! You've done OK!' In other words I didn't do too badly on earth. It was about doing your best. You don't have to be a 'Holy Joe'. 'You tried, therefore you are OK' was the message. It was amazing that this came across twice in exactly the same way. There wasn't one single difference. It was tremendous to experience that – it really was.

WILLIAM LACKEY, WHO COMES ORIGINALLY FROM COUNTY LONGFORD but who now lives in County Cork, describes what happened following a fall from a roof.

Some years ago we were putting pitch on a roof. It's a kind of tar and over it we would then put felt. The roof was 35 feet high. It was difficult to get to. You had to go in through an attic and then out through a window and onto the roof.

It started to rain. I shouted at the lads below and said, 'We can't work up here. I'm coming down.' I crossed one roof and came over to another one. There was a Perspex sheet in the roof. I stepped on it and it snapped. I went right through it and came down the full 35 feet, like a ton of bricks.

Everything happened so quickly. I came onto the floor in a store. I landed on my heels. I fell into a wheelbarrow. There were lots of wheelbarrows there, with their handles sticking up in the air. They were being stored in the room. Luckily enough, one barrow hit the other one over so I didn't hit the handle shafts. The barrow was twisted inside out with the impact of me coming down.

I went unconscious. Suddenly I was heading off and I saw a light in a tunnel. It was a fierce blinding light, flame coloured. I have never seen anything as strong. It wasn't like sunlight. Instead it was like a halogen lamp. The light was reflecting off everything. It was blinding me straight into my eyes. I felt I couldn't see.

The light was at the end of a long dark tunnel. The tunnel was only three or four feet wide. I was going through it and feeling my way along. It was very long. I couldn't see the end of it, it was that long. All I could really see was the light coming through from the end. I just kept going towards it. All my life I cycled a bicycle and I would keep cycling until I'd get to the far side of the mountain. It was a bit like that, heading for the light.

I felt very peaceful. I had no pain. I was wondering what was on the far side of the light. Suddenly the light went out completely. I thought I was gone. I said, 'That's it. I must be dying.' But I felt happy because I was so peaceful. I didn't care where I was going. Nobody spoke to me or anything like that.

Then the light came back on again for a while. I don't know what happened after that, whether it went out a second time or not. I don't know how I came around. Apparently the lads came looking for me. They had an awful job getting off the roof and getting down to where I was. But they found me and I was taken off to hospital.

After a while I came back to consciousness. Luckily I had no bones broken. But I was very shocked. And I had hurt my back badly. I was bruised. My whole body was twisted inside out. My wife said, 'Your face is sideways.' I had got such a bang on the ground that my body had twisted out of shape.

It took me a couple of weeks to recover. I couldn't move

and I had to sleep on a mattress on the ground. I couldn't go upstairs to bed. But I eventually got well. And I was so lucky that I hadn't hit my chin on a window, coming down from 35 feet. There were a few windows I could have hit. I just missed my chin by about one-half of an inch. I could have broken my neck.

Looking back, I'm sure I was dying. I never told anyone about seeing the light because I thought that people might just laugh at me. But I eventually read *Going Home* and I recognised what had happened. I realised that I was going to the other side. I also became happy about dying. It doesn't worry me at all. I don't worry about going and I believe I will meet my wife again whenever it happens.

TERESA, FROM COUNTY WATERFORD, went through her near-death experience during a traumatic time in her life.

We had a family gathering that took place in the late 1980s. It was a big event. It was very stressful. There was a lot of confusion. People came home from abroad and one or two of them stayed in my house. There was a lot of pressure.

Two days after the get-together I got violently sick. In the early morning I woke up feeling not so good. I had a dreadful headache. I said, 'Oh, my God!' I didn't know if it was the stress or strain. I came downstairs but I couldn't get sick. I went back upstairs again.

I was so bad that they got the ambulance for me. They took me off to the hospital. When the ambulance arrived at the hospital I was put on a trolley and wheeled in the main door. There were people pushing the trolley. I was then wheeled down a corridor. But it wasn't a corridor I was going down – I was going down a tunnel!

The tunnel was round, like a long drum. It was like metal.

It was coloured grey and it had rivets in it. It was like galvanised panelling. It covered everything and it went all around, from the floor up along the side, across the ceiling and down the other side.

It wasn't a particularly big or small tunnel. It was just big enough for me to go through on the trolley. I wasn't going either fast or slow. I was just going at a steady pace. I wasn't stopping. I didn't know where I was or where I was going. I couldn't see anyone on either side of me. I wasn't frightened. I heard nothing.

At the end of the tunnel there was a big black gate. It was an iron gate. It was like the front gate of a big house, with spikes and knobs on the top. It was high. While the gate was black, everything behind it was white. The background was like a bright, foggy light. It didn't blind me and it didn't make me blink. I was just staring at it.

I could see three people dressed in white behind the gate. They were completely in white. I could not see their faces. I thought they were angels. There could have been more there, I don't know, but all I saw were the three. Everything was snow-white, like a big ball of snow.

Eventually I got to the end of the tunnel. I couldn't say how long it took. As I approached the end, the gate was opening up and I was about to go through it. All of a sudden I heard someone saying, 'Teresa! Teresa! Teresa! Teresa!' My name was said several times. Suddenly I stopped and the tunnel disappeared. I never got to the white light. I saw it alright but I never got into it.

When I woke up I was in a ward and I was surrounded by doctors. They were bending down towards my face. They were calling me by my name and saying, 'Come back to us! Teresa! Teresa! Come back to us!' I opened my eyes. I was in a bed. The staff were rubbing my face and clapping me on the hand. I heard somebody say, 'She's back!' The doctors told me afterwards I had tears in my eyes.

They never really found out what had happened. They thought I had meningitis. They did a lumbar puncture. It was terrible. They did it once and it didn't work. They had to go and do it again. It turned out that it wasn't meningitis. They checked my heart but that was fine. They thought it was stress that had brought on the whole lot.

I know it was more than stress. I think myself that I just got so low that I had given up. I thought, 'This is the end! I can't take any more!' I know I was dying. I believe I was at death's door. Going through the tunnel I knew, 'This is it! I am going and I'm not coming back!' I also know if I hadn't heard the voice calling my name I was gone.

I will never forget what happened and it took me a long time to get over it. I told one or two people but I forgot about it after that. I don't speak about it now and I don't think about it either. I went to the priest to tell him. He said, 'Teresa, you weren't meant to go.' That's all he said. I think he was right. I was going to the other side but the man above wasn't ready for me.

HELENA, FROM COUNTY DOWN, describes her three near-death experiences. The first happened in 1999, the second in 2001 and the third in 2005.

The first one happened when I was in hospital with very severe abdominal problems. I had felt a kind of lump in my stomach. Eventually, one Saturday, I went into hospital. Before I left home I said, 'I'll have a shower first.' I went for the shower and I started vomiting blood. I went unconscious when I was in the car. It turned out that my large bowel had ruptured.

At some stage in the hospital – I don't know whether it was during the operation or in Intensive Care – I found myself in a transit lounge. I was going somewhere. I had come to what was like a gate you would find at an airport. There was this woman at a desk at the gate. I was being processed. I can't say I recognised her features but I knew she worked for an airline. She said, 'You have to sit there and wait on the side. We have to sort out some details.'

I sat and looked. There was this bit of a walkway in front of me. Behind it was a moving walkway which was made of glass. All of these people were going past me on the moving walkway. They were just ordinary people, dressed normally. There was a continuous stream of these people and they didn't appear to have any baggage. They seemed to go on forever, right to the horizon, which was very far away. They never noticed me at all and there was never any kind of acknowledgement.

I felt I wanted to go to where they were going, wherever that was. I was so anxious to join them. I couldn't understand why I couldn't go. It seemed I had to be picked up, that somebody had to collect me. But then there was a problem. This lady came back to me and said, 'I'm sorry but there has been a computer error. You can't go.'

With that I started to turn back. As I was turning I glanced back towards the distant horizon for a moment. Suddenly I saw my father, who was dead. He was coming towards me. He came on the walkway which was close to me. He was coming one way and the people were going the opposite way on the other walkway. He held his arms up and his hands were open towards me. He was waving to me. He was happy. I was happy to see him too.

Unfortunately I had to come back. I was sad but I did return. After that I have no idea what happened. I was unconscious for quite a few days. I can't even remember how long I was in the hospital. I eventually got better. Sometimes I question what happened and I wonder what caused it. But I never forgot it. It has stayed with me ever since.

The second event happened about two years later. My husband and I were in the car. He was driving and I was in the passenger seat. Another car was coming towards us. We collided slightly sideways. I took the brunt of it. I was very badly hurt. I had fractures, my spleen was fractured, my liver was damaged, my diaphragm was damaged and I had a massive internal bleed. I was a mess. My husband was OK because he had an air bag. But a little boy died in the other car and the father was badly injured.

At some stage I was going to a light. It was a beautiful white light. I was moving but not quickly and not in a hurry. It was like I was sliding forwards. It was like somebody else was transporting me. I was face first and very calm. It was the kind of calmness that you don't find in this world. I then heard the words, 'It's in God's hands now!' It was like an echo. The words were echoing in my head.

I was getting much closer to the light but then something happened. It seems like I wasn't ready to face it. It might have been some kind of guilty feeling, maybe something regarding the little boy who had died. I just don't know what happened. It was like I went into a black cloud or a wall or something. And I never got to the light. I just came back to myself in hospital. I was in hospital for six weeks and I never properly recovered. But, again, I never forgot what happened.

The third time I had gone on a visit abroad, to where I was born. I was due to come back to Northern Ireland. At breakfast I didn't feel very well. I excused myself and said, 'I'm going to lie down for a few minutes and get ready for the journey.' My brother said, 'You're not going anywhere.

You're going to see a doctor.' Apparently my eyes were kind of turning upside down in my head. I went to a doctor and he sent me to hospital. Before I knew it I was in Intensive Care. I had septicaemia. I don't know how I got it.

I remember nothing at all of what happened next. But I experienced something strange. I was walking on a farm and there were rows and rows of trees with white stems. There was light coming through the pale green leaves. The leaves were filtering the light. There was a shadowy green colour everywhere. I don't think I have ever seen light like that before. It was a most gorgeous day. Everything was most beautiful.

I was walking – almost dancing, because I was happy – through this landscape when, suddenly, my grandmother came and she sang a song to me. I never saw her. I just heard her. She sang a folk song like she used to sing to me long ago. She sang one verse. She then started fading away. I kept saying, 'There is another verse to it.' But she never came back.

I started looking for her but all I could see were the white stems of the trees. I wondered, 'Why did she disappear? Why didn't she finish the song?' I never remember what happened next. I can't recall coming out of that landscape. The next thing I recall was I had come back to myself and was awake.

All three experiences have had an impact on my life. There was a sort of feeling to them that I don't get in real life. It's a very pleasant feeling. They were wonderful experiences. But, while it is wonderful to be alive, death does not hold any fear for me. I don't fear death at all. When it happens it will be like a release.

In the meantime I have this strong urge to live. I have travelled a lot. I am happier in myself. I have a sort of drive now which I never really had before. I did have drive before but it was different. My life has been transformed and has got much better. Things have totally changed. I'm alive and I now get a lot out of every moment.

DEIRDRE COYLE, FROM COUNTY DUBLIN, describes how her son David appeared to undergo a series of near-death experiences before he passed away in April 2002. He was aged 17 when he died.

My son got sick at the age of two. He developed an extreme form of juvenile arthritis. His joints were very swollen and he would scream with pain. He had to be hospitalised for a while and had to have medication. He had a calcium imbalance and he eventually started to fracture.

When he was about nine or ten the arthritis went into remission. It had done its damage. Then he developed a skin disorder. It was a type of thickening of the skin. It lost its elasticity. His joints weren't able to stretch and grow. So he was very small and he was eventually in a power chair.

He put us all to shame, the way he would enjoy his life. He was always a happy kid, full of fun and extremely intelligent. He went to school. He would play hockey even though he would hardly be able to move the stick. There was nothing he wasn't able to do. He was lovely, just beautiful.

We were eventually told to take every day as it came. We didn't know when he was going to go. We were told he could go anytime. We made the best of it. We all went to Florida together. We went to New York. But, in time, I could see that his system was slowing down. I knew he was fading.

One night I was washing his teeth in the bathroom. He was on my lap and I was helping him do it. We were nearly finished. He suddenly passed out. He just dropped back in my arms like he was dead. He went as white as a ghost.

I said, 'Oh, my God!' I gave him a shake. He said, 'I'm

coming back! Don't worry, Mum! I'm coming back!' I could see the pink colour coming back into his cheeks. I thought it was strange but I didn't pay much attention to it. It was a shame that I never asked, 'Where did you go?'

About a month or two later I went away for a weekend with my friends. My husband Louis was looking after him. Both of them were watching a film together and there was just the two of them in the house. David decided that he was tired and wanted to go to bed. My husband decided that he would go to bed also.

Eventually David called out, 'I think I'm going to be sick.' My husband picked him up and he brought him into the bathroom. He started to get a bit sick. After one bout of it he stopped. My husband was waiting for the next dose to come but he suddenly noticed that David was still. There was no reaction from him at all. He was sort of frozen. It seemed to last for an eternity but it was probably only 20 or 30 seconds.

My husband realised that David wasn't with him anymore. He shook him and said, 'Come on, David. What's the matter?' He did it two or three times. Suddenly David shuddered a bit and he said, 'OK! OK! I'm coming, Dad!' That was it.

At the time my husband didn't want to frighten him by asking him about what had happened, thinking he might have been unaware of what had gone on. So he didn't ask him about it. David then went back to bed and eventually fell asleep.

Later on, when David's nurse came to visit him – he had a regular nurse who came to change bandages and do things like that – he was chatting to her about what had occurred. It was then that he said he had been in a tunnel heading towards a very bright light. His nurse asked, 'Were you frightened or scared?' He said, 'No. I was perfectly happy.' The nurse also asked him, 'Why did you come back?' He said, 'I heard Dad calling me.'

The next Tuesday night, four days later, I was putting him to bed and he said, 'I don't feel great. I don't feel well.' I said, 'I'll stay with you.' So I stayed with him until about one o'clock and he fell asleep. We were hardly in bed when, at three o'clock or so, he called us again.

We went into his room. He had gone white and passed out. You could see that the colour had gone out of his face. My husband Louis lifted him up and, having seen what had happened before, he said, 'He'll be OK. He'll come back.'

But he was struggling to come back. You could see the colour going out of his face. When he was coming back, you could see the flush returning and then he would go totally white again. He was gasping. His eyes were bulging. He was going white and he was going pink.

He was clearly trying to stay with us. Suddenly he said, 'It's not fair! It's not fair!' When he said that, it was all so clear to me. I said, 'OK! Davy, go!' And he died. It was 16 April 2002. He was aged 17.

Looking back I feel what happened was that he was being called by his relatives. They were asking him to come. I think they said that night, 'You have to come now, David. This time you have to come. This is the third time.' I think he was talking to them and he was saying, 'It's not fair!' I think what he meant by that was, 'I can't come. I can't leave Mum and Dad.' He was trying so hard to stay with us. You could see the struggle going on.

What happened has strengthened my beliefs a great deal. I believe our souls end up in the spirit world. I think it's a beautiful place. It is heavenly. As human beings I think we can't even imagine the beautiful joy and peace that's there.

I believe our relatives are there and they are waiting for us.

I think my son isn't with my parents but with Granddad Coyle and Granny Coyle. I believe they are looking after him. They were very caring. And he was close to them. They lived down the road from us and he was back and forth to them all the time.

As for the rest of us, we will never forget him. He was a wonderful boy. He was just beautiful. He had a great time. In the 17 years he lived he got more out of his life than we did out of ours. I know a lot of people say there are special children but my little fellow was a saint.

MARY FLYNN, FROM COUNTY KILDARE, had a near-death experience in 2005, replicating her mother's experience 30 years earlier.

In 1975 my mother, Mary, had a strange experience. I was only 28 at the time. She was up in St. Vincent's Hospital in Dublin. She had a heart problem and she went in for tests. She got a massive heart attack in the hospital. Her heart stopped.

On one occasion, after she got back on her feet, I remember my deceased husband and I were walking down a long corridor on either side of her. She pulled back her dressing-gown and she said, 'Look at my chest. It's black and blue. They must have danced the hornpipe on my chest.' She really didn't know the full extent of the trauma she had been through.

She then said, 'Do you know something? Wherever I was, or whatever happened, I was in this tunnel. I was spinning in the tunnel. I don't know where I was. I don't know how long it lasted. But I came to beautiful bright lights. Your father, Phil, was close to me. He was so close I didn't want to come back.'

I was surprised by what she said at the time. People wouldn't have been reading books on things like that in those days. There wasn't any real coverage on television about those sorts of things. She wouldn't have known about them. I was amazed.

She was the only one I ever heard talk about this sort of experience or the possibility of another life. But it confirmed to me and my brothers that there is definitely a life hereafter. I figured, 'My mother was dead. She died and was so close to being gone across the great divide.'

In 2005 – exactly 30 years later – I was in hospital myself with heart problems. I was in Naas Hospital for a month, waiting for a procedure to be done. Strangely, every other night I dreamt about my mother, who was dead at that stage – she had died three weeks after her near-death experience back in 1975. She figured in my dreams so much.

In those dreams she was pushing me away all the time. That's not like a mother. A mother should be bringing you towards her rather than pushing you away. I could hear her voice in my dreams saying, 'Go back to Frank! Go back to Frank!' Frank was my husband. I couldn't understand the significance of that until later on.

Eventually I was taken to Tallaght Hospital to have the procedure done. They removed about a litre of fluid from my heart. They did the procedure on a Friday. On the Saturday and the Sunday people were in and there was great rejoicing. I was thinking, 'This is marvellous. I'm going to be going home soon.'

On the Monday night I set about going to sleep around ten o'clock. I could see the time on a clock in the ward. I was saying my prayers and thanking God for being so well. I was thanking my mother and all the angels and the saints that everything was so good.

I woke at three o'clock in the morning and I felt dreadful. I knew something was happening. I rang the bell. The nurse came in. All I can remember saying was, 'I feel dreadful.' I just slumped down in the bed and went into cardiac arrest. My heart stopped and I went unconscious.

Suddenly I was head first into a tunnel. It was a round, dark tunnel. It was black. I was spinning round and round and going deeper and deeper. I was going down. It seemed to be getting shallow. I didn't see bright lights. I didn't get that far. When I eventually came back I could clearly see myself. If I shut my eyes now I can still see myself in that tunnel. I was definitely there.

Then I wakened up and it came to an end. It was twenty-to-four and I was surrounded by a team of consultants and cardiologists and whatever at the end of the bed. They were working on me and trying to get my heart beating again. I was so delighted to be alive.

It was only eventually that I put it all together by looking back to my mum's near-death experience, to my mother in my dreams in Naas Hospital and to my own cardiac arrest. I believe it was my mother who wakened me at three o'clock in the morning. I think there is no doubt although I don't know how she came to me.

People say, 'Sure, weren't you medicated?' People tend to put up a big defence arguing that there is no such thing. But I didn't know I was heading for a cardiac arrest. I believe my mother was my guardian angel. I think, being the maternal one, she was there.

A few years later, in August 2008, I lost my husband Frank to cancer. I didn't know I was going to have to face his death so soon after my own illness. But these are the things we have to live with. A strange thing was, when Frank was in a deep sleep before he died the one thing I noticed was that he would raise his left hand and reach out. I wondered, 'Who is he reaching out to?' I believe he wasn't reaching out to any of us around him but to somebody who had passed away.

Other people say, 'I don't believe in that.' But I certainly do. I believe we will see our loved ones once again. I believe I'll eventually see my deceased father and my mother and my husband, who was my best friend. I believe that people who've passed over, although we can't see them, they are there. I believe there is a life after death, without a doubt.

I'm not a 'Holy Mary'. I go to mass when I feel like it. And I'm part of my church choir. But I'm not into mediums or fortune-telling or anything like that. Yet I am sure there is a presence. And, although I can't see Frank, I do know he is there. I think it's all in a lovely prayer for those of us who have lost loved ones. It's called *Next To You*.

> You cannot see or touch me,
> But I'm standing next to you.
> Your tears can only hurt me,
> Your sadness makes me blue.
> Be brave and show a smiling face,
> Let not your grief show through.
> I love you from a different place,
> Yet I'm standing next to you.

JANE, FROM COUNTY DUBLIN, **recalls how her son had a life review during a choking episode he experienced in June 2005.**

My son had a head injury following an accident. It happened when he was 13-and-a-half. He had difficulty with a lot of things as a result. He had right-sided weakness. His balance was seriously compromised and he could fall over very easily. His memory was somewhat impaired. He had also lost the sight of one eye and had neurological problems with the other one.

He was in a coma for about 12 weeks. When he woke up

he couldn't walk or talk or speak. He was like a baby. He had to start again. Over a year in rehabilitation he learned how to walk and talk and speak and dress himself and do other things. But he never really recovered his sense of balance. About a year and a half after the accident he also developed epilepsy.

Throughout all this he battled away and went back to school. He did his Leaving Cert. and got onto a course. But it was a major head injury and he needed somebody with him and he needed a lot of support. Almost everything he did was difficult. Yet he was doing pretty well, despite the disabilities.

Nearly nine years after the accident he was doing a course but he had a day off. I said, 'Let's go out for lunch.' We went to a restaurant nearby. We sat outside, at a hard table, facing each other on the hard benches at either side of the table. I was looking into the sun and he had his back to it. He had a quiche and salads and I probably had a salad. We were sitting there eating and chatting.

I suddenly realised that he was choking. He didn't collapse and he didn't pass out. But it was obvious that it was really bad. I jumped up and shouted, 'My son is choking! My son is choking!' I ran around behind him and I did some sort of simulation of what one is meant to do in these situations. I pushed his tummy automatically, without ever even knowing I could do these things. He eventually coughed up a chunk of melon.

I then sat down beside him and we chatted. He suddenly said, 'I saw all the things of my life going before me. I could see my whole life in front of me.' I thought it was quite an extraordinary thing for him to say. It was as if he was telling me something that was quite surprising to him. He was very calm about it even though you might have expected him to be distressed.

What he said was particularly extraordinary because he wouldn't have been suggestible. He wouldn't have said it because it was something that other people might say. I also wouldn't have expected this to be something he would have come across. Instead I felt it was something completely from within. I felt that something really had happened beyond the norm. Unfortunately I didn't ask him what it was like and that was a big regret.

We then sat there for a little while. He settled down very quickly. I went and I picked up coffee. I was trying to be normal. And he was fine once again. But I felt that something unexpected had happened to both of us. It was certainly something unexpected to him. It's a pity, though, that I never asked him what it was.

When I came home that night I told all the family. I also said to him, 'You really gave us all a fright today and you gave yourself a fright.' I don't know that he was as frightened as I was. He was fine again. There was nothing strange. But I really felt he had brushed with death that day. I certainly felt it. It was like turning up a card, like the jack of spades was played that day, although that might only be hindsight.

Looking back, I don't know how long this whole thing had been going on for. We had been totally relaxed. Given that we were sitting there chatting and eating and looking around, it could have been going on for a minute or more before I noticed it. There was no sound because he couldn't cough. It could have been going on longer and he could have gone further than I was conscious of.

We might have forgotten this except that six days later he died. He had a seizure, which wasn't anticipated. It was a sudden, unexplained death. I felt the closeness of these two experiences was strange. I wondered had something happened back in the restaurant. Had it started then? Had something begun that he couldn't have stopped? Was he stepping over a line there? Was he beginning to leave us?

I wonder did he get a glimpse of something that day. I also wonder did it make it easier for him when the time came. Maybe he was happy to go when he went because he had an inkling of what he was going to. You could say it was all a coincidence. But I don't think coincidences really happen.

The memory of what happened has always been there. I can hardly think about him dying without thinking about a lot of things that led to the time it happened, including that. It was strange these two things happened within such a short time. It gave me more of a chilled feeling that maybe he was further along the line than I thought at the time. But that's what he said. My only regret is that I never asked him what it entailed.

SIMON POMPHRETT, FROM COUNTY CORK, had his near-death experience back in the 1960s. It happened following a serious car crash.

In 1967 I was in a car crash about two miles outside Gorey, County Wexford. There were four of us in the car. It was about one o'clock in the morning and we were heading from Enniscorthy up to Arklow. We were coming from the Fleadh Cheoil. We were going to stay with a friend that night.

We were heading into Gorey in a Fiat when a back tyre burst in the car. I think it was the left tyre but I'm not sure because I never saw the car afterwards. What happened was we hit another car that was parked at the side of the road. Our car was wrecked. It was eventually taken away to a scrap heap.

I was in the front passenger seat. Apparently I hit the top of the car and I was knocked unconscious. I was lucky. What saved me was that I was after falling asleep. A friend of mine, who was the driver, broke his pelvis. Another friend in the back seat broke his leg. The fourth fellow had concussion but that was all.

Suddenly, while I was unconscious, I felt I was out of my body and going away from it. I was going down a tunnel, heading for the other side. It was a big dark tunnel, a bit like a laneway or a dark alleyway. It was jet black, like a lane would be late at night with no light on the street.

My spirit was leaving my body. I thought there was no end to it. I was falling and falling and couldn't stop myself. I think I was going head first although I'm not sure. But I definitely was going downwards. Beelzebub must have been waiting for me that same night!

There was a big bright light down at the end of the tunnel. It was very bright, like the brightest white bulb you could get. It was way off, miles in the distance. I was heading towards it but I never got near to the light. I felt very relaxed although I remember saying, 'I don't want to die!'

I didn't meet anybody in the tunnel but suddenly, while I was in it, I was back at the crash scene and there were lots of people there. I was in a car, driving along and we came on a crash. I got out of the car to see what was after happening. There was a gang of people around the crash, standing there and looking at a person on the road. There were ten or twelve people there but I couldn't put a face on them.

The people were dressed in ordinary clothes, like they had been out for the night and had just come on a crash. It was as if they had stopped to look after the people lying on the road. They were bent over this person. I pushed my way through the crowd and looked down at the body lying there. That person was *me*, laid out flat on my back, like as if I was asleep. I knew I was looking at myself. I was shocked.

I blacked out after that. We were lucky because there was a nurse in the car behind us. She dragged me out of the car and rushed me into the hospital because she thought I was dying. I have a memory of her saying, 'Get him into hospital because he is dying!' I can recall that happening at the scene.

I don't remember being brought into the hospital because I was unconscious. I don't remember anything more after that either, although at some stage I do recall the doctor saying, 'He's alright! He's alright! We'll get him around!' He was beside me in the ward. But I don't remember anything else and I heard later that they thought I was gone.

When I woke up it was about nine o'clock in the morning. I was in this strange room and I wondered, 'What the hell am I doing here?' I had a big bandage around my head. The others were in the hospital as well. They were shipped out to a different hospital that day but I was kept where I was because they didn't want to be shifting me.

I remember, after I woke up, I got out of bed because I could hear my friends in the next ward. I was spotted and was rushed back into bed. I was still in a bad way. That night, at five-to-seven, I was anointed by a priest who came in.

After a week or so I was released from the hospital and came home. I never forgot what happened. I think I must have died that night. I think the doctor at the hospital believed that too. I think I was on my way to my 'Redeemer' but I came back. I think I was heading to the other side but I was saved by the nurse coming on the scene.

I think I was helped in another way too. A year beforehand two of my brothers had been killed in a gas explosion. A cylinder of bottled gas had exploded. One of them died on the day of the explosion. The other died two weeks after. I think they were looking after me, helping me that night.

Sometimes, when people talk about accidents, I tell them

my story and they say, 'That couldn't have happened.' They don't believe me. But I know it happened. And I have no doubt that I was heading to my 'Maker'. I still have the dent on the top of my head to prove it. It's there to this day. I was just one of the lucky ones who came back.

It is a happy memory for me. I'm happy I got over it. Later I had prostate cancer and I won that battle too and it's gone, thank God. But I don't worry about dying as I believe there is another place. I go to mass now, every day, and I believe there is a God. I believe there is a heaven I will go to when I die. There is somewhere we will all go to in the end.

CATHLÍN, FROM COUNTY CARLOW, had a strange near-death experience following an operation to remove her appendix. It happened in the 1980s.

I had a pain for two weeks and I thought it was nothing. One Saturday morning I was doing some work for my father and the pain became very sharp in my side. I said to my mother, 'I'd better go to the doctor.' I went to the doctor in the town and he said, 'It's your appendix. You've got to go to Kilkenny. You need to get it out.'

I went into Kilkenny. When I got there the doctor asked me, 'How long do you have the pain?' I said, 'I have it two weeks.' I really thought it was nothing but he said, 'We have to rush you down to theatre!' I had my operation and all seemed to have gone well. I was then brought back to my bed.

I was back in my bed for about 15 or 20 minutes when suddenly I started trembling with the cold. A fierce coldness came over me. I was shivering. I could see all of these doctors rushing all around me. I was saying, 'Oh! The cold! I'm freezing!' They were putting more blankets on me. Somebody came in with a big cylinder of oxygen and they stuck a big oxygen mask on my face. I could barely see them. There was a lot going on.

I suddenly thought I was drifting off, away from myself. I was in this place. I don't know where it was. It was like if you went into a forest where the trees were all grown over in the shape of an arch. I felt like I was going along this forestry walk under the arch. The walk stretched on ahead of me. It was like I was on this journey.

Next thing, down at the very end, I could see this blue. Everything was sky-blue. The place was full of light. It was very bright. It was like somebody had painted a room blue and then turned a big light on. There were white clouds there, floating around. They were floating by. I could see all this in the distance.

I had this rushing feeling. It was like there was a big wave of water and I was floating on top of it. It felt like I was being carried. I will never forget the peace. It felt like nothing on earth. It was absolutely beautiful. You really couldn't describe it. The best I could say is that it was like sitting in the garden in a chair with the sun shining on you. It was wonderful. The peace and tranquillity were unbelievable.

I also saw what I believe was Our Lady. She was dressed in blue. She looked beautiful, with a beautiful face. I think she had a flower held in against her chest. She wasn't very clear because of the light. She was blending in with the blue but I felt I could see her.

Suddenly I came out of it. When I was sort of coming out the nurse was there, waking me up. She was asking me, 'Are you alright now? Are you feeling better?' I felt the heat was back in my body. I felt warm again. I said to her, 'Oh! I was in such a lovely place!' She said to me, 'You were talking all the time. You kept saying, "Oh! Look at this place! Look at the blue and the clouds!"' She just kind of smiled. And that was it.

I must have been near death when all this was happening. They told me later that my blood pressure was dangerously low after the operation. The doctor also said that another day without my appendix being taken out and I would have been dead. So I was very lucky. But I definitely believe I was going somewhere. I bet you I was near death.

I felt different after it. I started to sense things. About 14 or 15 years ago I had an awful dream. Down in a field I saw the world burning up and a man I knew was burning up in the middle of the fire. I told my father all about it. A week afterwards that man was killed on a road. He was working on the road when a car came up behind him and killed him. I couldn't believe it. My father was shocked. He said, 'You were only dreaming about that man a week ago.'

I can also sense things. I can sense if someone is going to come to visit. I can sense if the phone is going to ring. And I always think about what happened that day. It just comes into my head, now and again, and I'd tell my friends about it. I can remember it as if it was only after taking place. I always feel good about it. And I always say, 'That was a lovely place I was in back in the 1980s.'

FRANCES CLARKE, FROM COUNTY DUBLIN, journeyed to the light back in 1970 following a childbirth that almost went wrong.

I was having my son by Caesarean section in hospital. It was an emergency. I was haemorrhaging badly and the consultant was called in to operate. Suddenly I must have left my body although I wasn't up on the ceiling and looking down or anything like that. I could, however, hear the surgeon who was operating on me. I was later able to tell him what he was saying and what he was doing. But I couldn't respond.

I felt myself drifting off. I was conscious of falling into a tunnel, going downwards and downwards. I was going face forward and heading downwards all the time. The sides of the tunnel were dark grey. It was like a whirlpool in the tunnel. But I don't know whether the sides of the tunnel were going around or whether I was going around.

I was heading towards a huge bright light. It was a very comforting bright light. The light got brighter and brighter as I got closer. I had a warm feeling. I wasn't afraid. I just knew I was going somewhere that felt right.

I got to the end of the tunnel. That's when I saw a big field with a whole pile of people in it. There was an awful lot of people standing and waiting for me. They were dressed in long white robes. I didn't recognise their faces, except that they all looked so happy. I wanted to be in with all of them.

There was somebody standing in front of them. He had long hair, with arms outstretched, and was also dressed in a white robe. His arms were outstretched for me. I didn't recognise that person either. All the time, the bright light was behind him. I was very, very happy to be there. I felt I was going home, really belonging.

I was then told that I had to go back, that I couldn't stay. It was just a voice that told me. It was a very kind male voice. The words used were, 'You can't come now! You have to go back!' I think it must have been the person out in front, with the arms outstretched, who told me. It was said very kindly but no reason was given as to why. So I never crossed over.

I was devastated. I didn't want to go back. I wanted to go on because everything was so happy and so peaceful. I felt so totally at home and so loved in a way I never felt before. There was a great feeling of belonging. It felt very spiritual. Everything was just right, pure and without stain. It was beyond anything I ever felt here on earth. I would nearly say it was 'heavenly' even though at the time I wasn't given to religion or to anything spiritual.

That's where it ended. I did come back. I don't know how long my experience lasted. I just suddenly returned to the ward and I was unconscious for possibly another day. I was then hooked up to drips and whatever for the rest of the time. I have no real details of what happened to me, from a medical point of view, except that I almost died. You never asked in those days. You felt you had no right. You just got on with it.

My husband couldn't be contacted at that time. But the consultant did tell my mother. She came in the following day although I couldn't talk to her. She ran screaming down the corridor because of what had happened to her daughter. They told her, 'We nearly lost your daughter last night.' It transpired that I had to be brought down to the theatre three times that night and I had to be given blood transfusions.

To this day I haven't found out a real meaning for what happened. I ended up thinking that every second person had an experience like this. However, somewhere along the line, someone said to me that it must have been that my work on earth wasn't finished.

I have become a really spiritual person, especially in the last ten years or so. I have learned that, in my own personal disappointment and struggles with various aspects of my life, everyone is on their own. In addition, I have noticed how so many wonderful people have been sent my way and who help me out.

I am also happy to die. My father lived to a great old age and he was terrified to die. I used to try and console him and tell him there was nothing to be afraid of and that he would be very happy. Nothing I said would get through. But, for me, I'm not a bit afraid because I know there's something there.

I know there's something ahead of us and I'll be happy to be there.

OLIVER, FROM COUNTY LOUTH, had one of the earliest near-death experiences I encountered. His experience occurred in 1957, almost two decades before the phenomenon was first identified and categorised in the USA. He was aged 22.

I was an able-bodied seaman in the British Merchant Navy. In 1957 I was on an oil tanker, the *San Vulfrano*, which was owned by Eagle Oil. We were off West Africa and we were going over to the West Indies. I think it was Haiti we were heading to. When we were off West Africa I wasn't feeling too good. I was kind of coming and going into a coma. I had malarial fever before and I thought that's what I had.

We got to the Caribbean and we then made our way back to Scotland. I got another attack of this sickness. I thought it was the malarial fever back again. I finished up going to a place called Irvine, in Scotland, where they had a fever hospital. They didn't know what it was. They treated me for malaria and gave me quinine. But it transpired later that I had typhoid fever.

I died at one stage in the hospital. I died for two minutes. Suddenly everything seemed to be white and I was climbing a big white ladder. It was like a wobbly Jacob's ladder, like you would use for climbing on a ship. It was very white, a very bright colour. I was heading upwards, going slowly enough. The ladder was surrounded by a very pale bluish colour. There was nothing else to be seen. I was just trying to get to the top of the ladder.

I then looked up and I could see this person – a man or something – with his long arm out, calling me and trying to bring me along. He was dressed in white, with a white beard and white all over. He kept calling me, putting his hand out and waving me to come up to him. I could see his mouth being formed as if he was saying, 'Come! Come!' He was putting his hand down towards me as if to give me a hand.

I felt very good about what was happening. I felt very happy. I wanted to get up there. I didn't mind climbing the ladder because I was used to climbing them anyway. I wasn't worried about doing it at all. But I never got to the top. I couldn't hold on. I kept sliding back down again. I couldn't make it. And that's how I came back.

I didn't realise what had happened at the time. It was only afterwards that one of the doctors in the hospital said that I had died. When I woke up she said, 'You came back to us!' I said, 'Why? What do you mean? Where was I?' She said, 'You left us for two minutes.' I said, 'What do you mean by I "left"?' She said, 'You were dead for two minutes.' She told me they had pronounced me dead.

The doctors then asked me all kinds of questions. They were asking me, 'What did you see? Where did you go?' I told them what had happened and I said I thought I was just having a dream. But they said, 'No. You weren't just having a dream. You were bodily dead.' They also told me they had to send for my mother to come over. But by the time my mother arrived I was OK. I was in the hospital for over two months and I gradually got well again.

I couldn't explain what I had just been through. It was hard to explain. I said it to people at the time and they just laughed at me. They said, 'When you're dead you're dead!' They thought it was very funny. This sort of thing wasn't known about at the time.

I didn't know what to call it at first. I thought initially that it was a 'dream' or a 'trance' or something. But I've thought about it a lot since. And I know it wasn't a dream – it was real. It really happened to me. It definitely happened.

I can still remember it today, crystal clear. The memory is always there. It will never go away. I often think about it. And I often think about what it would be like to go off again like that. But, after what happened, I wouldn't be afraid.

I am not afraid of death. I wouldn't worry about dying tomorrow, if that's what dying is like. I say a few prayers every now and again. And I know that when I die it's going to be something like that. There's nothing to be afraid of. It's going to be very peaceful up there.

GERARDINE, FROM COUNTY WATERFORD, **had what appears to have been an out-of-body experience. The out-of-body element, although it can happen on its own, can also be the first stage of a near-death experience.**

It happened in October 1983. My now-husband and I decided to bring my sister and her husband out for a meal to celebrate their wedding anniversary. We took them for dinner and we were having a lovely meal. I didn't feel well. I said, 'I'm just going outside the front door to get some fresh air. I'll be back in a minute.' Once I got outside I fainted and I was on the ground.

Suddenly I floated up and could see myself down below. I was overhead and looking at myself. I was on my right side, lying across the doorway. I probably naturally had gone into a recovery position. I had also got sick. I was up above, just over the head of the doorway, to the right-hand side of where I was lying. I thought, 'This is weird! How am I up here? How can I be seeing myself from up here when I'm down there?'

The feeling I had was like a warm glow. It was a warm, lovely feeling. It felt like I was inside the warmest quilt that you could ever imagine. I was so cosy although I was lying on a cold concrete ground. I was happy. I didn't want to be waking up because it was so lovely.

It was like as if you were down in Spain and lying out in the sun on a nice comfortable bed. If you'd shut your eyes for a moment you'd get this lovely feeling of the heat penetrating your skin. For a second you might drop off to sleep. That was the feeling.

Afterwards I had four children and the loveliest thing in the delivery ward was that they would come along with this blue blanket and they would wrap it around you because your body would be a little bit in shock. You'd feel, 'This is so cosy. I must have died and gone to heaven.' It reminded me of the feeling I had back in 1983 – of being in a warm place, with a warm quilt around me.

Then it was over and it was all so quick. It just finished. They all came rushing out because I wasn't coming back. As I came around I thought, 'Why am I waking up? This is so nice.' When I saw the actual condition I was in I wondered, 'How could I have felt like that?'

I never actually said it to the others that night. I felt so embarrassed. I thought, 'If I say this it will sound so weird.' I also thought, 'Maybe it didn't happen anyway.' I mentioned it once or twice but nobody took any notice. I felt, 'I'd better not be saying this to anyone, anymore, because it's so stupid.'

Yet I never forgot it. It must have made a big impression on me because I have always remembered the date and the year. But it's only when I read *Going Home* that I said, 'Oh, my God!' I wondered, 'Could something more have happened to me if somebody hadn't come out and found me?' I suppose I'll never know. But, whatever it was, it was lovely.

PATRICIA PLUNKETT, FROM COUNTY MAYO, similarly went through the initial stages of a near-death experience before suddenly returning to her body. It happened in the late 1970s.

I was in a serious car crash back in 1978. I was only 20 at the time. I was on my way down from Dublin to the West on a holiday. The accident happened near Mullingar, at around four o'clock. I was in the passenger seat. We were coming to a bridge. I could see yellow-and-black lines on the bridge. I said to the driver, 'Slow down! You're going too fast!' I knew, at that point, we were going to hit something.

I put my hand on the dashboard and we hit a Land Rover coming towards us. I hit the windscreen and bounced back into the car. It was the September before the seatbelt law came into force. The Land Rover didn't even get a dent but our car was completely written off.

I was left with chronic facial injuries and I also lost a lot of blood as well. I had a neck injury and my knees were damaged. I also ended up with a back problem. The person who was driving me was grand. He only cut his ear. My two sisters were in the back and none of them had any injuries although one sister doesn't remember a thing.

People got out of their cars. The next car behind us had a nurse in it and she helped. Then the ambulance came. They got us to the hospital. I stayed conscious throughout. They put me into Intensive Care. I remained conscious for a long time. My sisters were allowed to come and sit around the bed. Eventually they were moved out and the curtains were closed around me. I can remember being cordoned off and isolated. After that I was gone.

I suddenly felt myself slowly floating upwards. I couldn't feel anything and I wasn't in any pain. I just floated higher and higher and everything below me got smaller and smaller. I looked down and I saw a funeral. I saw a church, a coffin and people kneeling down. I could see the pews but I couldn't identify anybody. Yet I knew it was me in the coffin.

I could hear prayers being said. I tried to join in the prayers but, although in my head I could say the prayers, my mouth wasn't able to mutter the words. It was a funny sensation. My voice just wouldn't come out of me. I wasn't happy because I wanted to pray. I just kept saying to myself, 'Why can't I join in on these prayers?'

At the same time I was being drawn further and further away from where I was. I was floating way up into the sky. I was going higher and higher. The people below me were getting smaller and smaller. I didn't mind being up in the air. It was a nice sensation even though I hate flying. I knew I hadn't got any control at the time. I knew I couldn't bring myself down. I was just up there knowing it was me down below and wondering why I couldn't participate in the prayers.

I then felt myself saying, 'I don't want to go! I have too much to do!' I had always wanted to be married and have a family. I really wanted to have children. That was my ambition. So I said, 'I haven't finished what I want to do!' I knew I wasn't ready. With that I willed myself back down again and I went back into my body. It happened all of a sudden, in a flash.

My eyes suddenly opened. I was wide awake and this priest was anointing me. The priest was putting the oil on my forehead. There were two nurses and a doctor at my bedside and each had a rosary beads. They were all saying the rosary and they were crying. I knew immediately where I had been heading. I said to myself, 'I was gone!' It was eight o'clock in the evening.

I was transferred after that to Dublin so I never got a

chance to ask the nurses or the doctors what had happened to me at that point. I often thought about trying to find the records yet I never did. But I think I definitely had died. I am sure that I was at least dying, if not dead, and moving on. It just ended early possibly because I wasn't ready and because I wanted to come back and finish something.

I believe there's no question that I was on the first stage of a near-death experience. I was definitely heading somewhere beyond this realm. I didn't see bright lights or a tunnel. And, at that stage, I didn't feel a presence of God. But I did after I came back. It changed my faith. I had a more fearful faith back then. I have a lovely faith now. I now feel my faith is deeper and I have grown a lot.

I also feel, since then, that I have a purpose. As I said to myself at the time, 'I will live on because I have a family to rear.' Eventually I did get married although I didn't meet my husband until six years later. And I now have my children. I have four of them. So I feel everybody has a purpose. I feel, even now, that I still have a purpose and I'm not ready to go. I believe I still have much more to do.

GINA LAWLOR, WHO COMES ORIGINALLY FROM COUNTY DUBLIN but who lives in County Galway, had a strange experience back in the mid-1990s. On the surface it appears to have been an out-of-body experience although it also contained elements of a near-death experience – including the bright light, the witnessing of a deceased relative, the sound of a reassuring voice and long-lasting after-effects.

One night I was lying in my bed, awake. It was around ten or eleven o'clock. I was just resting while settling down to sleep. Suddenly I felt this sort of 'pull', which went down through my feet. It was very strange. I wondered, 'What's happening?' I was completely surprised. I sort of screamed out loud. But I was conscious that my son was over in the other bed and I didn't want to wake him up.

I was suddenly pulled out through my feet. I felt a weight had been lifted and I was floating up. I ended up about the height of the wardrobe. It felt very high. I looked down and I could see myself lying in the bed. I also saw Christopher, who was about seven at the time. I saw he was still asleep. I wondered, 'What on earth am I doing here?'

Then I saw a sort of yellow light. It was very radiant. It was like the amber light you'd see at traffic-lights. It was coming in from the bottom of a very large window which was near Christopher's bed. It was coming through the curtains. It was night and the curtains were shut. It was the top floor of a building and there was no other light coming in.

Next I saw a man standing at the side of Christopher's bed. He seemed to develop from the light. He just seemed to appear from it. He was wearing a black suit. To me, a black suit either implies a priest or my grandfather who wore one. At the time, however, I wasn't thinking about my granddad. I just saw this man standing at the side of the bed and he had his hands behind his back. He was looking down towards Christopher.

I saw the back of the man. I was up behind him. Although I could see the back of his head, I can really only remember the suit. I got the impression that he was fairly old. I didn't feel any threat even though the idea of a man looking at your child would, you would think, make you go, 'Oh, God!' I had no sense that this was a bad thing or a bad feeling.

Later on, when I told Mum and Dad about what had happened, Mum reminded me that Granddad used to walk down the garden with his hands behind his back, surveying his vegetables. She reminded me that he always wore a black suit. We thought, 'That's weird!' But, even though I didn't think of that at the time, I didn't feel threatened at all. I was very calm. I also felt very free and very light.

The next thing I heard a voice. It was a male voice. It wasn't old or young, just middle-aged. The voice and the man didn't match. It was in my head and not physically in front of me. It said, 'Everything is going to be OK! Everything is going to be OK! Everything is going to be OK!' The voice sounded knowledgeable. I don't really know what it meant. Maybe I just needed to be told that everything was going to be OK in my life. I have no idea.

With that I was back into my body again. It felt like I came back in as soon as the message was said to me. I said, 'Oh, my God!' Immediately after it happened I remember being out of sorts. I rang my sister straight away. I also told my parents. They were quite religious. My dad told me, 'Go to a priest.' And I did. The priest said, 'You are not the only one who has experienced things like this. If it wasn't threatening or bad then take some good out of it.'

But I wondered, 'Why me?' I was just an ordinary person. I wasn't sick. It wasn't anything to do with being in hospital. I didn't have a drink. It was just an ordinary evening when I was settling down. People said I was hallucinating but I wasn't. Some people scoffed at me. But, over the years, I have often said, 'I don't care what people think because I know what I went through.' I felt, 'This is my story and it's not to be laughed at.'

Looking back, what I took from it all is that there is something beyond where we are. I also took from it that we don't die. Maybe some people have this shown to them. I eventually read up about it and came across lots of explanations – like when you sleep your body separates from your soul and you can become aware of that separation. But I just accept it as it was and I can't put an interpretation on it.

The experience was actually very comforting. I found it precious to me. I didn't belittle it by telling it to everybody. But it certainly led me to being more spiritual. I feel I am a better person for it. I was brought up strictly but I am more open now to other beliefs. I have a more open mind now. And I think we are more than just a body. Maybe that's what the purpose was – to show me that.

ROISIN FITZPATRICK, FROM COUNTY WICKLOW, had a most remarkable experience shortly after she haemorrhaged on 22 March 2004.

It all started on the day after my thirty-fifth birthday, at a quarter-to-two. It was a beautiful Monday afternoon. I was all on my own. I was listening to some music. Suddenly a horrendous pain appeared at the back of my head. I had never experienced anything like it before. My neck went into severe spasm and it pulled my head backwards. I then began vomiting and feeling hot and cold sweats. I felt extremely weak.

I knew immediately I either had a brain haemorrhage or it was meningitis. It was so severe that I knew I could die. I figured that out. But I was very cool and calm. I remained conscious and I was able to call an ambulance. I said, 'I need help!' They arrived and brought me to the hospital.

Initially I was in A&E but later on I was transferred to another hospital and put into Intensive Care. I was told by the doctor, 'You have a high risk of dying or having a stroke and being paralysed for the rest of your life.' The enormity of the situation dawned on me at that stage. I knew by then that I had a brain haemorrhage. I knew that I had to stay calm to survive. I shed a few tears of raw emotion.

What happened next was literally the most amazing experience of my life. It happened within half an hour of my arriving in Intensive Care. I started to feel pulsating, undulating waves of energy flowing throughout my body. I could see the waves visually with my eyes. I could feel them. All that existed was this infinite, pulsating vibration of pure energy and I was keying into it. I was part of it.

I experienced a blissful ecstasy. It was like every part of my being was overwhelmed with bliss. It was a state beyond the mind, beyond happiness or joy. I felt great serenity, peace, love, harmony, calmness and oneness. This was a whole new dimension to anything I had ever been familiar with before.

I saw vivid waves of colour – purples, greens, blues, violets, everything. The colours were all very vibrant, very alive. There was a lot of beautiful light. But it was about more than the colours and the light. It was about being part of this energy and I could feel it on every level with my senses. There was nothing to compare it to.

It was not like I was in my body anymore. I felt I was part of something bigger. My body wasn't relevant. It didn't matter if I returned to my body or not. There was no sense of a start or a finish. The most overriding feeling was of infinity, that life was continuous and never-ending. It just went on and on forever, in every direction. I also realised that there is no such thing as life or death. Everything is all one.

I went in and out of this state over a few days, during which I had more experiences. On one occasion I had the sensation of being held in the palm of God's hand. I was very small, curled up in the foetal position and being held in this enormous hand beneath me. It was really a spiritual God and not the God we know of from different religions.

I got a very strong feeling to let go and to surrender to this God, who was wonderful, compassionate and beautiful. I felt totally safe, totally protected and completely supported. The words that came to me were, 'Surrender to the bliss!'

On another occasion I was surrounded by a vast, infinite, calm turquoise sea. The sea was an iridescent colour and it was sparkling. It was really clear and vibrant. It's so difficult to describe the vibrancy. I was on this little wooden pier and I dived in. I went down and down and down. There was no end to it. It stayed the same colour the whole way down. Eventually I came up and went into the sky, which was the same turquoise colour. It felt there was no depth or height that you couldn't go beyond. There was this sense of infinity.

On a further occasion I was walking through a winter's garden. As I walked by, it became springtime. Everything started blossoming. All the flower beds and shrubs came alive. In particular I remember a very beautiful cherry blossom tree with stunning pale pink flowers which opened up. An old mansion was there. The house became restored and beautiful. To me it was like the energy was bringing everything alive.

I had these experiences over about two or three days. Then I gradually got physically better. As I did, all my senses were heightened. There were fluorescent lights in the hospital and they were excruciatingly painful. My sense of smell was also affected. The chemicals, such as the bleaches they use in hospitals, were like an assault on my sense of smell. Every sound was heightened. You can imagine in a hospital, with the trolleys and noise, what it was like.

They told me that I'd had a brain haemorrhage. It took a good six months to a year before I came back to myself again. But it was never really back to normal. The energy was still with me. I wanted to integrate it into my body, and I did so. I still felt sensitive and, to a certain degree, that sensitivity remains. For example, I find it very challenging to look at all the violence and wars in the world and on computer games.

I also integrated this sensitivity into art. I became an artist. Light became central to my work. I held that as my focus – the idea of being 'artist of the light.' People respond to it. Light isn't threatening to anybody. Some people feel a sense of peace and stillness. Other people feel incredible joy when they are standing in front of the pieces. More feel the presence of relatives or friends who have passed over. I am very fortunate that I can now channel this light through my art.

Looking back, I believe I had a near-death experience. What happened arose from being literally near death. I was on the edge. I also had my experience with God. I had the sense of peace, connection, blissfulness, and it had such a dramatic impact on my purpose in life. Life became very simple and very clear. And I have absolutely no fear of dying.

I now focus on living life and enjoying every moment of it because there is no death. I know I am part of something bigger, a vast consciousness, something greater than us all. I also have an inner compass and strength and they always point me in the right direction. That's the best way to describe it. With the light, life flows beautifully. I connect with that place and I just know what the right thing is to do.

Eithne, from County Cork, seemed to witness her father's near-death experience back in 2003. She contacted me having spotted the similarities between her story and those related in my book *Going Home*.

I wasn't actually dying at all. Nor was I in any way near to death. Instead my father was dying back in 2003. He was in his late 80s, pretty elderly and he'd had heart problems for many years. He'd had his ups and downs. But this time it became clear, over the five days or so before he died, that he was not going to come back. He was going downhill fast.

He was in hospital and I would be with him every day. I would visit and spend a lot of time there. I was very like him and very tuned into him. We were cut from the same cloth. However, I wasn't religious in any way. But my father had a very strong faith and was very committed in a real way. He was a genuine Christian. He was terribly sure about where he was going and very calm about it. I was not so sure at all.

About two days before he died I had this extraordinary experience. I was at my father's bedside. It was morning time. I was the only one visiting. I was standing beside him because they were short of chairs. He was lying in the bed, right in front of me. He was frail and had an oxygen mask which he had to keep on. He was just lying back on the pillows.

It's difficult to describe what happened. Suddenly it felt like I was in this 'vastness'. It was as if there was a vast landscape around me, extending to infinity. It was really huge but not frightening. It was welcoming and comfortable. I heard a voice or a message saying, 'This is reality! This is reality!' I didn't know what it meant. I still don't know.

Then I was in a sort of a cave or a tunnel, which was reasonably big. It was kind of cinematic in effect. I was standing in the wings, at the side of this cave or tunnel. It was kind of lit up although there wasn't a light at the end of it.

My father was to my left and in front of him, facing him, was this doorway or aperture or opening. Beside that was a sort of screen with pictures. I remember looking at the screen although I didn't really see the contents. It was like a life review. It was going on in front of my father. I knew instantly what was going on although I had never seen it before.

Again I heard a message like in 'surround sound'. It said, 'It's yourself you have to face!' I was thinking, 'Yes. You have to face your whole life and review everything you've done.' I was saying, 'Yes. That's it.'

Then I looked over at my father and he was facing this review. He had this look on his face. It was lit up and he had this smile. It was a kind of a blissful look. There was this aura of glowing happiness about him. I thought, 'He would be happy because he was always moral and he has always done the right things.'

Then I heard another message, 'He knows!' I didn't know what it was about. Was it that he knew what he was facing? Was it that he knew this was his death? Did it mean that he was OK with it? I really don't know. It was just, 'He knows!' I was mesmerised about what was going on. My jaw dropped with shock.

I then heard another sort of 'surround sound' message coming at me and saying, 'Everyone should be like this!' That was the end of it. Then it was over and I was back in the hospital ward, with my father right in front of me. I don't know how long it all took but my feet were still on the ground. I was where I had obviously been all along. I was in the same position. So it can't have taken long.

I left at lunchtime and I got into the car. I turned on the engine and the radio came on. It was the one o'clock news with Seán O'Rourke. He was interviewing somebody to do with corruption and bank accounts and with moving money around and all that. He was really getting his teeth into this. Whoever he was interviewing was fighting back.

All I remember thinking was, 'None of this really matters.' I felt, 'How small our everyday stuff is. It's so small in comparison to death, which is the biggest moment in your life. This is the one timeless moment into which everything collapses. Compared to it, everything else is really nothing.' I thought, 'There's no need to get worked up over everyday stuff. It becomes so unimportant in the end.' That has stayed with me. It changed my life, in that sense.

My father died about two days later. It really wasn't until a while after he died that I wondered, 'What on earth was that?' In the weeks and months afterwards I'd be going for walks with my dog and wondering what to make of it. I was trying to figure out what it was, what it meant to me and what I got from it.

I would often ask myself, 'How did it happen?' I still don't know. It seems I tuned into what was happening with my father. Somehow or other, I became an observer in my father's death process. From the stories in *Going Home*, they would all seem to be broadly similar and they might have been what my father would have gone through. They all seem to go through this process and go through a tunnel opening. So, given that my father was going through his death process, somehow or other I got to be in the wing watching it.

I don't know how that would happen. I don't believe it was an overactive imagination. I guess I was within the range of 'normal' for somebody whose parent is dying. It's never easy but I wasn't overly stressed.

I have queried myself about if I imagined all of this because I was so worried about my father dying. But I would have to have had a hell of an imagination to come up with this. If my imagination is that good I should be writing *Harry Potter* or something!

It was hard to tell other people because many might say, 'My father died but I never experienced that.' It's not that they would doubt me but they might feel, 'How come you got to see this death process?' I also knew people might ask if I was drinking or whatever. But I barely ever drink and I've never smoked tobacco never mind taken anything else. I wasn't unwell or on any medication or on mind-altering substances of any kind.

I don't have any fear of death now. The idea of it doesn't

scare me. When somebody dies I don't feel that it is something absolutely tragic. Don't get me wrong, I would hate it if my own children died. But, in general, I feel this very positively-charged feeling about death. I am also left with the feeling that everything is so small compared to this huge, enormous thing that's awaiting us. It is a good feeling.

Finally, I got a sense of how important it is how you've acted or behaved in your life. I knew that my father lived a very good life. But I felt, 'I'm not ready for this. I've got to improve myself. I should be better than I am.' That's a thing I have tried to work on. You've really got to be as good as you can be so that you can face yourself. It's how you live day to day, and the choices that you make, are what matter.

OTHERWORLD VISIONS

In my book *Going Home* I describe how the Irish author and playwright Hugh Leonard received a visit from his deceased wife Paule shortly after she died. 'I walked into the living-room and she was standing facing the fireplace,' Leonard recalled. 'Before I could blink she was gone. It was as if I had caught her when she didn't mean to be caught. I can tell you what she was wearing. I can tell you exactly the turn of her head, absolutely everything. She was there, solid as anything, and then just went.'

What I omitted from *Going Home* was that the author had another visitation – this time from his dead mother. It happened one day, back in the 1960s, while he was living and working in the UK. Unlike the earlier vision, this one occurred on the borders of sleep when, as Leonard put it, he was 'caught between sleeping and waking.'

'I was inside a garden,' the author – who died in 2009 – said. 'There was a white gate. She came up the outside. She was wearing a hat that I had seen in a photograph, an old photograph, a kind of a cloche-type hat from the early '30s. She came up and she lectured me in a sort of impatient way about detaining her when she had other things to do and other places to go.

'The strange thing was that I was not outside the gate. I was inside, as if I were at a remove. She was outside. She was the free one. She could go where she liked. Then she went on her way. And she went along this path.'

As with other people's experiences, Hugh Leonard's two visitations were substantial and appeared to be real. In that sense they were distinctly unlike 'ghosts', which are often described as being ethereal, misty or having the appearance of human breath. The events also involved people who were familiar and known.

One visit happened in the course of Leonard's everyday activities, while he was fully awake. The other occurred as a 'bedroom visitation' – a category covering happenings that normally take place either before or following sleep. Both followed closely after death, reflecting the trend for many visitations to occur in the weeks or months after a person passes away. These core characteristics are evident in a large number of the stories that follow.

Many of the narratives involve loved ones returning to reassure those left behind that they are happy and at peace. The departed occasionally come back to offer help in times of danger or need. In other cases they warn of pending tragedies, primarily deaths.

Sometimes those who are dying report seeing dead relatives or friends coming to welcome them to the other side. These are referred to as 'death-bed visions'. Finally, the visitations may be hostile although this is rare. All of these categories – with the exception of hostile apparitions – are featured in this chapter.

WESLEY, WHO COMES ORIGINALLY FROM COUNTY MONAGHAN, was visited by his wife on two occasions following her death.

Back in 2008 my wife died from a massive heart attack. She had been sick for a while. She had gone into hospital. She was really only going in there for a preparation and the following weekend she was planning on going to a function. I had been in with her and she was in full spirits when I left.

The following morning I got a call to say I should get to the hospital immediately. When I got there she was alive but they wouldn't let me see her. There was a team of doctors working with her but within minutes they told me they had lost her. It was a great shock because we thought she was well on the way to recovery.

We had the usual formalities and funerals and all the rest of it. I got through them all and faced up to the new realities. I had to settle into the habit of an empty house. Anybody would find it tough. It was also tough that there had never been any goodbyes in any shape or form. Her death had been so unexpected.

Sometime, in the first two months, I was asleep in bed and I wakened up. It was early in the morning. It must have been around five o'clock. It was probably in mid-October. I sensed there was something strange in the room. I don't know whether it was a sort of coldness or a presence or whatever.

I had been lying on my right side, the way I always sleep. I turned over and sat up in the bed. I looked around me. There she was! My wife was over at the door, down at the bottom of the room, about 20 feet away. She was crystal clear. She was life-sized and dressed in a dressing-gown. She started walking towards the bed.

She was smiling. She looked very happy. For a second or two I forgot that she was dead. I didn't speak but I put my hands out. She turned slightly to my right – or to her left – to where the door is. And she was gone. The whole incident probably lasted about 10 or 15 seconds.

I wasn't shocked. Instead I was comforted. I had no fear that I had seen a ghost or that anything supernatural had happened. I'm also convinced I was 100 per cent awake and that it wasn't part of a dream. I was, after all, sitting up. And I remained awake for a while afterwards. I just felt that she was there to say, 'I'm happy and I want you to be happy too.' I lay back down into the bed and felt a really warm happiness.

It happened once again, on another occasion, when I was abroad. I was in a place where we had been on holiday before. It was a very bright morning, in clear daylight. Again, for no reason whatsoever, I sat up in bed. The door was in the corner of the room, to my left. I looked straight through to the door. Once again, there she was!

She stood there and looked in the door. She was standing there, slightly leaning back. She was dressed in a suit, with a tidy little skirt and jacket and a blouse. She smiled. This time I spoke. I said, 'Come on in. You are very welcome.' I remember my very words. Being the second time, I was a bit more confident about looking and talking and staring. That's probably why I was able to speak.

She walked towards the bed. I was almost within touching distance. It was almost as though we were about to have a laugh together. But, before I could touch her, she disappeared. This time I expected her to go. It lasted for about the same length of time, maybe fractionally longer, about 20 seconds. Afterwards I just lay back down in bed again and enjoyed the wonderful sensation of having seen her.

Both events are still very vivid in my mind and I will never forget them. In both cases she passed me from the left to the right. On the first occasion she came towards me slightly from the left and then disappeared to my right. On the second occasion the door she came from was slightly to the left and she walked straight towards me but again she disappeared to the right.

There's nothing that makes me think they were part of my imagination. There was definitely something I felt in the room and it was responsible for waking me up. It wasn't like I was half asleep or anything like that. I'm convinced I was awake. I wasn't lying around waiting for her to come into the room either.

I've only told a couple of close friends but I wouldn't have told them if I believed the events hadn't happened, if I thought they had been a figment of my imagination. I've only told a few people because most people would either laugh or say I was hallucinating. But I believe that what happened was real. My own honest view is that, on both occasions, she came back to let me know she was happy and to see that I was OK.

Also, in both cases, I felt a great comfort. This is the one thing that came through very strongly. I would have always felt that if I saw a ghost, or anything like that, I'd have fear. But I had no fear whatsoever, none at all. Instead, I will always remember the smile and the look of contentment, the image that she was totally at peace with herself and with me. I will also remember the feeling that she was happy and, for the few moments she was there, that I was sharing time with the person I loved.

BELLA, FROM COUNTY DONEGAL, describes another straight-forward visitation, this one involving her mother and her aunt. It happened on 3 February 2007.

My mum lived with me for ten years. She was in her late 80s and had Alzheimer's. She was wheelchair-bound. She wasn't really with it. One Saturday, in February 2007, I was in the kitchen in the back of the house, sweeping the floor. It was late afternoon, around four or five o'clock. My mum was in the sitting-room in her wheelchair, watching the television. She was only six footsteps away.

Suddenly I heard her calling out, 'Teresa! Teresa! Come here! Teresa! Come here! Come back!' She kept calling out the name. Teresa was a sister of my mum, who was living in Northern Ireland. There had been 11 in her family but she and Teresa had both been nurses and were very close. They had trained together and there was just two years between them.

I went in and I asked her, 'Mummy, what's wrong? Who are you talking to?' She said, 'Teresa was here but she is away.' I recognised immediately who she was referring to. My mum wouldn't have seen her for a few years. I also realised from the way my mum called out that she really felt she was there. I said, 'Teresa is not here. I'm the only one in the house.' But my mum said, 'She was here.'

I finished sweeping the floor and I went into the sitting-room. I just sat down and started reading the paper. Suddenly Mammy got sick all over the floor. She didn't get sick very often and there was no reason for it. I got up and started cleaning the carpet. I was down on my knees when the house phone rang in the sitting-room.

I think it was one of Teresa's daughters on the phone. She said, 'I'm sorry to tell you that Mammy has passed away.' Her mother, Teresa, had just died ten or fifteen minutes beforehand. I made the connection immediately. I was absolutely stunned and flabbergasted. I was shocked.

It's not as if Teresa was spoken about daily in the house. She mightn't have been spoken about in a month or two months. There was no indication that she was sick and I wasn't aware that she was dying at the time. There also was no other Teresa locally who would have been calling in or out to the house.

I think my mum, who later died in 2008, must have seen her sister. I am sure Teresa was there. I mean, my mum, with her Alzheimer's, wouldn't have thought about her sister in a long time. And it couldn't have been a coincidence that she mentioned her at the exact same time she died. So I believe Teresa certainly did come back to see her sister or to say goodbye.

NEWSREADER ANNE DOYLE recalls how her brother, John, was visited by their deceased mother shortly before his death from cancer in 2000.

I can remember very clearly, back in early September 2000, I was at an introductory workshop of the RTÉ Authority, which I had been elected to, and I got a phone call at the end of it. I was told that my eldest brother, John, who was living in Wexford, had collapsed and gone into hospital. That was the first news I had that he was unwell and, as far as I know, that was the first time he was aware that he was ill.

It turned out he had multiple myeloma and it was in the final stage. He must have been feeling some tiredness or weakness. But myeloma very often doesn't give any other indications. So if you're not somebody who gets regularly checked, the illness could be very advanced. There was never any hope. He was 58 at the time.

What was most strange was that a relatively short period before this happened – within just a couple of weeks – my brother Tom was up from Cork visiting the lads, including John, at home. This was at a stage when nobody was aware that there was any problem. John was out with his dog, walking him down the field. It was a sunny, hot August day. He came back into the house ashen faced. He was as white as a ghost. He said, 'I saw Mammy down the field!'

Tom was there, with a couple of them, and they said, 'What do you mean?' My mother had died in 1979. He said he was just walking along, in the long grass, and he saw what was like a freeze-frame of my mother. It looked like a picture of her. It wasn't my mother as a three-dimensional woman standing in front of him. It seemed to be one-dimensional. And she was looking straight at him.

It was nearly like she was in a picture frame, although she wasn't, and he was aware that she was looking at him. She didn't say anything. She just looked. There was nothing said. This was with the sun scorching down, at about two or three o'clock in the afternoon. He hadn't been drinking or anything. In fact, he had given up drink altogether even though he never really drank very much. He obviously got a hell of a shock.

It was a very short time afterwards, just a few weeks, when he collapsed. He was brought into hospital in Wexford. I went down to see him. My brother Tom had told me separately about what had happened. So I asked John about it because obviously I was astounded.

He described this one-dimensional effect and he said, 'It was Mammy and she was looking at me.' I said, 'How did she look?' I really don't know what I meant but I think I meant, 'Did she look young or old?' He thought I was asking about her expression. He said to me, 'She looked concerned.'

I asked him, 'What do you think it was?' He said, 'I don't know. She was just there, looking at me, and she looked concerned.' It was an unusual word for him to use. I said, 'Do you mean like worried?' He said, 'Yes, she was worried.' To my knowledge, if he did put that together with his illness he never mentioned it and it wasn't the kind of thing you would wish to mention to him in case it would alarm him.

I believed it although I found it very hard to get my head around it. My brother Tom, who is a sensible kind of a fellow and quite a reflective person, also believed it. He was quite sure. I didn't even have a question mark at the time although I suppose if nothing else had happened to John we might have been left with a question mark. But I didn't dwell on it at the time and we all talked about it as if it was a matter-of-fact thing.

After that, John was transferred to hospital in Waterford and he was then back and forward to St Luke's. I spoke to the haematologist in Waterford and I understood the prognosis immediately – there really wasn't any hope for him. While I was aware of his prognosis, John wasn't although he was no fool. He was dead by November.

There is absolutely no doubt that John saw my mother. I believe that my mother came to her boy. She was a very strong woman and I believe she came to John because he was facing a very unpleasant death. As the youngest of the family I would have probably been my mother's pet. Anything that ever needed handling by way of responsibility in the family would have been looked after by my second-eldest brother because he is sensible. But John was Mammy's first son and she, like a lot of mothers, loved her first son. John was the apple of her eye.

I absolutely believe that he saw my mother. I have no reason not to. My belief is that her concerns for John were such that, somehow or other, I don't know how, she came to him. She must have known that he was not going to have a very good time because, obviously, the vale of death can be fierce.

If it had happened when he was in hospital or attending a doctor or been ill I would have said to myself, 'He was probably concerned or bothered or worried about things.' It also wasn't like he was rolling back from the pub and saw an apparition up the road. That would be a different matter. But this was just a sunny summer's afternoon walk in the lush grassy lands of Coolatore. There was nothing amiss. The last thing that was on his mind was that he was going to see my mother. There was no reason for that to happen.

If somebody else told me, I'd be disinclined to believe it. I'd be saying to myself, 'There must be some piece of information, or piece of the puzzle, that the person is missing.' But, as a result of this, I believe that death isn't final. It's not what I would have believed before. My thinking has been changed completely. That's because I believe that what happened did really happen. And I don't believe it because I want to believe it. I believe it, full stop.

MARY, FROM COUNTY LOUTH, recalls how she was visited by her younger sister who had died in a fire.

I had two sisters and a little brother who died in a fire back in April 1977. It was a house fire and it was awful. My older sister was going on 12 and my little sister was going on 5. My little brother was going on 8. Another brother survived.

I was 21, the oldest, and I was married and living in England at the time. It was heartbreaking. When I got the phone call I was told that everyone was gone, Mammy and Daddy as well. But my parents survived and one of my brothers also.

In the early summertime of the following year, around May, Mammy was supposed to be coming over to visit me but she got an offer to go to Lourdes. It must have been around May because that's when everyone seems to go to Lourdes. I got the phone call to say she wasn't coming. I felt disappointed. But I didn't think much about it.

A few months later, in July or August, my sister Patricia appeared to me. I had been sleeping but I awoke and I saw her at the bottom of the bed. She wasn't really standing or floating – she just seemed to be risen up a bit. She was kind of hovering but it's hard to explain.

I had a big bedroom, with a double bed, and my little boy was in the bed with me. There was a huge window, the length of the wall. The curtains were open because I was in a flat on the third floor. So it was bright and I could see my sister clearly. Even now I can see what she was like at the bottom of the bed. I can still see her the way she was when she came to me.

She was about the same age as the last time I had seen her, about 12. She was life-sized. But she wasn't in normal clothes and her hair was different. She was wearing like a white, flowing dress and her hair was shorter. I wondered why her hair was shorter because she had lovely long hair when she was alive.

Everything was white – her clothes and her face – but her hair was black. There was kind of a light around her. It wasn't a bright light, more like a glow or an aura. She didn't seem scared. She was just Patricia, my sister.

I didn't say much but I did ask her, 'Are you OK? Are you alright?' She said, 'Yes. I am happy.' She told me they were all fine and not to worry. I also asked her did she meet Nanny and Granda. I had been very close to them and I wondered did they come to bring her to the other side. She said, 'It was Nanny and Granda who came to take me.'

She said, 'Mammy will be alright because she has her work and her friends.' She also said, 'Daddy won't be too long before he joins me.' She said he couldn't cope. As it happened, my father didn't last long afterwards. She then said, 'Before the day is out you are going to get a surprise.' I looked at the clock and it was six o'clock in the morning. When I looked back she was gone.

I had a wee son and a job and I used to take my son to work with me. I was able to do that where I worked. I got ready and just as I was passing the phone to go out it rang. It was Mammy and she said to me, 'Hello, Mary. I've got a surprise for you.' I said, 'I know. You're coming over.' She said, 'How did you know that?' I said, 'I just know.' I knew because Patricia said I was going to get a surprise before the end of the day. I thought, 'That has to be it.'

Looking back, I don't believe it was a dream. I feel I was really awake because I turned and I looked at the clock. In fact, I know I was awake. I know people thought I had lost the plot, when I told them, and they probably still do. People thought I was a crackpot. They thought I was from a different planet. But I don't say it to many people. And I don't care what anybody says – I know it happened. I know it is true and I know I saw her.

I think of it all the time and I still can't understand why she came to me. Maybe it was because I always got on well with her. I suppose I looked after all of them a lot, especially when Mammy had been out at work. So we were close. But, whatever the reason, when something happens like what happened to me you think, 'There's got to be something.' And I definitely believe there is something else there.

TOM, FROM COUNTY CORK, was visited by his deceased mother and aunt. It happened back in the mid-1980s, when he was in his 40s.

In 1986 my mother died. Her name was Teresa. I had been very close to her. My father had already died from T.B. I was only a year-and-a-half old when he died so maybe there was a special bond there with my mother. I think everyone is close to their mother anyway. So I was taking her death very badly. I was grieving a lot.

About a month after my mother died, I was in bed one night. It was about three o'clock in the morning. It was just a normal night. My wife and I were both asleep. My aunt Kitty suddenly appeared at our bedroom door. It was like it happened in a dream. She was the youngest in my mother's family and had died a few years beforehand in Cardiff, where she lived.

My aunt Kitty was smiling. My mother was behind her. She was looking over my aunt's shoulder and she was smiling too. They both appeared at the same time. They both had radiant smiles. I felt my mother was happy. I felt my aunt was happy too.

My aunt, who was at the front, was dressed in everyday clothes. I could see all of her. She was dressed well. But it was mainly my mother's face that I saw. She was behind Kitty, who was taller. Kitty was in her way. It was like my mother was looking over her shoulder so that I could see her. It was also like Kitty was saying, 'She's with me. She's alright.' That's the impression I got.

The bedroom light and the landing light were on so I could see both of them clearly. I don't recall ever leaving the lights on. I could see that everything was in colour. You could make out the colours of their clothes. They both looked about the same age as when they died. My mother was 72 when she died. My aunt was in her 60s. My aunt had fallen and broken her arm. On her way into the hospital she had died from the shock. She had been close to my mother.

I think I fell into a happy sleep afterwards. When I woke up the following morning, I talked to my wife about it. I believed it was a dream. She felt I hadn't been asleep but that I had actually seen them. She told me afterwards that I changed completely, that I suddenly started accepting my mother's death. She thought it made a huge difference.

I had something similar happen to me with my mother-in-law. She had died back in 1982. Her son Donal had died long before that, back in the early 1960s. He was only ten when he died. Eventually her husband Dan, who was my father-in-law, was dying in hospital. I stayed a night with him. I was beside him, dozing off in a chair. I was sitting facing the door and he was behind me.

Suddenly I saw my deceased mother-in-law at the door. She was wearing a sort of camel-coloured coat. She looked good and fresh. She looked across me and spoke to her husband. She said, 'Donal is waiting outside. But you're not ready yet. We'll be going on ahead. We'll carry on.' Dan didn't die that night. It was the following night when he died.

I did tell some people about what happened on both occasions and they believed me. I also believe these things can happen. I think there must be some sort of contact with people who have passed on. I also think that people come to you. I believe they come to let you know they are OK. And I think it would be an awfully sad life if we didn't meet our relatives again.

In the case of my mother and aunt, I was very happy that I saw them and that I got that message. I felt Kitty was really saying to me, 'Don't worry. Your mother is with me.' I think, after it happened, I was happier in myself and came to terms with my mother's death. I accepted it. It also made me feel that if the likes of them weren't in heaven then there can't be a heaven. What harm did they ever do to anybody?

What happened on both occasions are not things you take lightly. They had a big impact on me. The details, in my memory, don't change over time. They remain the same. They stay vividly with me. I later had a heart attack and every minute of that day sticks with me as well. Some things happen yesterday and you can't remember them at all. But certain things stick in your mind. And these are things I will never forget.

LYNN BUFFINGTON, WHO LIVES NEAR THE CORK/LIMERICK border but who comes from the USA, explains how her deceased brother, Edward, appeared to her one day in her car.

My brother passed away suddenly on 6 July 2007. We were extremely close. There was only 18 months between us. We could understand each other. We could communicate with a look or a glance across a room. He would also turn up when and where I needed him. So, even though he was in the States and I was in Ireland, it was like we were never separated.

I got a phone call from him on 4 July. It was a big holiday in America and I was here. We ended the conversation with 'I love you.' As I left the phone, I got a weird feeling that I wanted to call him back. I thought, 'That's crazy.' He was on his way to a picnic. I said, 'No. I won't call him.' So I didn't.

Two days later, at about one-thirty in the morning, I got a phone call at home. It was my other brother and my sister on the line together. They asked me if my husband was here. I said, 'He has just gone up to bed.' I was watching a movie with a friend of mine who was down visiting from Dublin. My sister said, 'I want you to get him. I need him to be right there with you.'

I knew something was terribly wrong but I assumed that one of my nephews had been in a car accident or something. I never thought of my brother because he was only 50 years old. My husband came downstairs. He went on the phone. He said, 'I'm so sorry! I'm so sorry!' He just looked at me and said, 'Your brother has passed away.' It turned out that he'd had a massive heart attack. I literally, for the first time in my life, understood the idea of being struck with grief. I collapsed. I really didn't think I could breathe.

Anyway, I went home to the States. We had a private

service for him. He was cremated and we went out on his best friend's boat to take his ashes to sea. We poured a bottle of Jack Daniel's in, because that was his drink of preference. It was beautiful. I sang some songs and I had with me a compilation tape of songs that meant a lot to him and me together. One of them was 'He Ain't Heavy, He's My Brother.' That was like my tribute to him. We played that and some Beach Boys songs too.

I returned to Ireland. Then, about a month after his death, I was sitting in my car getting ready to drive home. It was daylight. It wasn't raining. I had just left work at around five o'clock. I wasn't tired. I didn't have a late evening the night before. I wasn't on tranquilisers or anything. I was just going through the ritual of fastening the seatbelt and adjusting the mirror and everything else.

I had popped a CD in and it was the Beach Boys. I loved it. It was good driving music and it was a long drive home. But it wouldn't play the Beach Boys. It kept playing 'He Ain't Heavy, He's My Brother.' I kept taking the CD out and putting it back in. I was looking at the cover trying to figure out what was wrong. But it was definitely a Beach Boys CD, with the correct and original label on it. Yet, every time I played it, 'He Ain't Heavy, He's My Brother' kept coming up.

I was in a parking-lot at the time and I stopped the car. I put my head on the steering-wheel. I remember rubbing my head and saying, 'Oh, my God! I think I'm having some kind of a breakdown. I need to talk to somebody.' I mean, I was going through a stressful time. I thought, 'This is getting serious. I need to go for some help.' I said to my brother, 'I hope you're not messing with me. Is this a sort of sign or something?'

I then turned to my left and he was literally sitting in the car. He had a red shirt on and jeans and his Dockers boat shoes. He was smiling and happy. He had his arm over the back of my seat, which he always used to do. I was just sitting there. It lasted a good five seconds. It wasn't just a flash. I had enough time to turn to him and see his smile and smile back. I had time to recognise what he had on and that he was healthy and happy.

I got a surprise. I didn't say anything. I just smiled. But I got what it was about. I think it was his way of letting me know that he didn't want me to be sad. He didn't want me to continue to mourn and be upset. It was his way of telling me, 'I am home safe and I will always be here for you.'

I was in a horrific crash about a week after that. I was down in a ditch, with the car upside down. The car had flipped three times. It was a complete write-off. I was upside down in the car before a farmer found me and pulled me out. I literally should not have been able to live never mind walk out of my car.

I know my brother protected me. I was fine even though the car was destroyed. Everything in the car was smashed including all the CDs – but not the Beach Boys CD. It wasn't even in the CD player. It was in a sleeve and the other 23 CDs in that sleeve were destroyed.

I know he came back to me. It's more than a belief – it's a 'knowing'. And I feel blessed because I have that 'knowing'. Also what happened to me when I saw my brother in the car was wonderful. It was so reassuring. It was definitely one of the most amazing things that ever happened in my life.

PAT STOREY, FROM COUNTY DOWN, **had a visit from her deceased husband shortly after his death in August 2001.**

My husband, who was 75, had been diagnosed with bowel cancer. We had been up at the hospital one August day. It was a Wednesday. The oncologist said that, with treatment – chemotherapy and radiotherapy – and also an operation, he was 99 per cent sure that everything would be absolutely OK. We came home in the car. My husband said, 'Are you happier now?' I said, 'My goodness. Yes. Are you not?'

He came home that day and he worked in the garden. It was a lovely afternoon. Our garden faces south so he said, 'Why don't we have a drink before we go in?' He wanted to get the last of the sun. We had our drink. Then we had our meal and sat about. I went on to bed, as usual. He followed and got into bed beside me. Everything was absolutely normal.

I wakened an hour or so later. I heard this awful breathing noise. I said, 'Are you alright?' He said nothing. Our own doctor lived just across the road from us. So I phoned and he came over. Unfortunately my husband was gone. He'd had a massive heart attack. I phoned a niece and she came over and stayed with me. That was early on the Thursday morning.

Throughout the Thursday I was in complete shock. I just couldn't believe what had happened. One minute he was there and the next minute he was gone. That Thursday morning I gathered his things together for the undertaker. We had gathered together his shirt and things like that. I said to my niece, 'What about shoes?' She said, 'No. He won't need shoes. I asked the chap and he said that you don't need shoes.'

I went to bed as usual that night. On the Friday morning I woke up at about eight o'clock. We had a bungalow. There was a big window over on my left. It was a floor-to-ceiling window, looking out on the garden. I was just lying there, looking out. I was wide awake. Suddenly Alan was there, over to my left. I could see him as clearly as I can see the table in front of me as I am talking to you now.

There was a dressing-table next to the corner of the window and he was between the dressing-table and the window. He was standing up and dressed in the clothes I had left out for him. He had a nice pair of grey trousers on and a white shirt with grey-and-red stripes. He had a grey-and-red striped tie. I could see he was in his stockings. He looked very happy. He was exactly the same as he was before he died.

He said, 'You forgot to give me shoes, Pet!' He always called me 'Pet'. I said, 'You don't need them, Love.' He said, 'That's OK!' Just with that, my niece knocked on the bedroom door and came in. Suddenly he was gone. He wasn't there anymore. I said to my niece, 'You've just missed Alan. He was here.' She sat on the bed. I told her what he had said. I don't know whether she thought I was hallucinating or something.

Looking back, it was all very real to me. I know other people think it wasn't. I didn't tell people at first because I wondered what they would think. People have said to me, 'You were sleeping. You were dozing. You were dreaming.' But I know I wasn't dozing or dreaming. To me it was terribly real. I was wide awake.

I now feel a warm, comfortable feeling when I think back. Having seen him like that, I knew that he was at peace. His only concern was that he didn't have shoes. At his funeral, other people were coming in and they were crying. But I was saying, 'Don't worry. He is at peace. He is happy.' That's how I remember him now. When I see him now, I just see him there at the window and I know he is at peace and so happy.

TONY, A FARMER FROM COUNTY CAVAN, describes how his deceased son reappeared in 'special dreams'.

Anthony was my only son. He was 21 years of age. He was starting his third year in college, doing an art and graphics degree. He had incredible artistic ability. He was very good with clay and working with his hands. But he also expressed an interest in farming. I think he might have worked on both sides of it – the farming and the art.

In September 2005 he went out on a Saturday night with his friend. They went to a disco. On the way home, at about three or half-three in the morning, their car went off the road on the top of a very slight hill. It went through two fences. It overturned and then righted itself.

Anthony had been in the passenger seat and he was thrown out of the car. He landed about ten metres away. He was alive when the driver got to him. But he died very soon after in the field. It was absolutely horrendous. It was indescribable the effect it had on myself and my wife and his five sisters.

A couple of months later Anthony came back to me one night in what I call a 'special dream'. Firstly, I felt there was a very holy man in front of me, dressed in black. I didn't see his face. I reached out to touch him. Suddenly Anthony sprang up between me and the man. He said, 'Hi, Dad. I'm back. I'm just back to let you know I'm in an incredible place. You're going to love it when you get here.'

He was dressed in normal clothes but there seemed to be a glow around him. It was a yellowish glow. He was lit up and in wonderful humour. When he was alive he would have tinted his hair a bit but that was all gone and he was very normal looking. His hair had gone back to its original colour. Immediately after speaking to me, he was gone.

I call what I saw a 'dream' because it happened in the middle of the night. If it had happened when I was awake, during the day, I would call it a vision. Although I tend to regard it as a dream, it was a very special one. It was very different in comparison with the normal dreams we have every other night of the week. In this dream you can smell, you can feel and you can see.

I recently came across a woman in America who had the

same sort of dreams. Her son was thrown from a car and killed as well. He came back to her twice. She also calls them 'very special dreams', where she could smell, feel and see. I believe that what we both experienced was the same. I think that's how Anthony came back to me – through my dream. I think that sort of thing does happen.

A week later he came back to me again. He was sitting on a step of our stairs and I was sitting on a step below him. It was daytime. This time he was more natural than the first time. There was no light or aura around him. He was again dressed in normal clothes. Because I was sitting below him, I was turning my body around to look at him.

He said, 'You know, Dad, it's like being back in college. I'm studying an awful lot.' I think that when we die we have an awful lot to learn – things that we will be taught and shown – and I think that's what he was referring to. That was the end of it. Then he was gone again.

My wife had one too. There were a lot of young men in her dream, all dressed in white. She recognised Anthony, who was also in white. She said, 'Anthony, I'm going to get the car and bring you home.' When she went back to him she couldn't distinguish him. That was her dream. It was very profound for her too.

What happened has meant everything to me. The dreams were a huge consolation, especially for a man who believed life was finished as a result of a tremendous blow like ours. My reaction has been incredible peace and contentment. And I know that Anthony is safe. I believe that somewhere in there the Almighty had a hand in it. I really believe that. I think he allows these things for consolation.

The dreams have also convinced me that there is another world out there and that there is life after death. I think that in these dreams I have seen it. All down through the Old

Testament and New Testament, people have trusted and relied on dreams. I'm inclined to do that now. As a result, I believe Anthony is in heaven. And I believe that one day I will meet him and be reunited with him again. I just can't wait.

EIMER, WHO COMES FROM COUNTY KILKENNY, outlines what happened when her father died in early 2009.

My father had emphysema and was 88 at the time he died. Emphysema can be an awful thing. It can be very distressing and frightening. His lungs were completely gone. Things got so bad that he couldn't get his breath. He was completely dependent on oxygen. I think he knew what was coming.

We would all take turns minding him at home. There was always somebody there each weekend. Near the end he got one infection after the other. His immune system was shot because he was on so much medication. He became very distressed and he couldn't get his breath. He developed pneumonia. He had to be taken into hospital by ambulance.

The following Tuesday afternoon I went in to visit him. I sensed a big change. I think he knew it himself. I said to him, 'Daddy, when you do go I want you to give me a sign that you're still with us.' He turned to me and said, 'I'm not ready to go yet! Finnerty and Naughton are getting the place ready for me!' They were two of his childhood friends who had only died in recent years. I wasn't at all shocked. I assumed they had made some connection and they were getting his resting-place ready.

On the Wednesday I was with him again, along with other family members. He suddenly turned to me and to his niece and said, 'Dad is calling me!' He said it in a very matter-of-fact way. His dad had died a long time before. His niece raised an eyebrow at me. But, again, I wasn't really surprised. I had an acceptance that this was all just part of what goes on.

I also felt my father deserved whoever was coming to him before he passed over.

I also knew there was something unusual going on in the room. It was tangible. There was something happening in the air. The only way I can describe it is that it was as if little threads were being woven. It was like there was some sort of energy there. It was like a 'sizzling' in the air, movement all around. I couldn't see it, yet I was sensing it.

Early on the Thursday morning I was with him once more. He looked great that day, maybe about ten years younger. We were all saying a few prayers. When we were finished he said, 'There are spirited priests at the end of the bed!' He was still lucid, completely conscious. One of his friends was there and she just looked at me. I had no fear.

We stayed with him 24 hours a day over the following days. Then, on the Monday, it started snowing. I was at home with my mother. My sister rang at about 11 o'clock. She told me that Daddy was still breathing but was after closing his eyes. She rang again around lunchtime and said we should get to the hospital. After we arrived my sister and I said some prayers. We whispered them to Daddy. We held his hands. And at twenty-past-two he died.

The snow was still falling when we brought him home on the Tuesday. It was like as if the world stood still. Everything was so gentle and calm. There was a genuine beauty around. Although I was still in shock, there was a great sense of peacefulness. We then buried him on the Thursday.

The following Sunday I arrived home and went to bed exhausted. It was almost a week since Daddy had died. I had the most incredible dream. My mother, sister and myself were in this big room in my dream. There was a coffin in the room, with a lid on it. There also was a ceiling-to-floor window, with ceiling-to-floor curtains that were half-open, halfway pulled back.

Coming across the glass of this window was my father's hand. It was really his arm from the elbow down. I knew it was his hand. His hands were so beautiful. He was knocking on the glass. I got a fright and I started crying. The hand pulled away. Then he knocked again.

Immediately Daddy was standing in the room with us. He had a long white robe on him and it was tied around the waist. It was Daddy as he looked 40 years ago. He had lovely strong features and very dark eyebrows. There was a yellow-red-orange glow all around him. With that, my dream ended.

The dream didn't wake me up. I didn't open my eyes and see him in my room. But, when I woke up in the morning, I remembered what I had dreamt. It's as clear to me today as it was then. And I believe it was Daddy coming to me and telling me he is OK where he is now. It was him coming to me and giving me a sign, as I asked him to do.

What happened around my father's death gave me great comfort. It was so comforting and lovely, so beautiful. It has deepened my feelings for my father and my need to honour him for bringing me into this world. He was such a good man. I now love to go in and light a candle to him in the church, and I like going to mass.

Looking back, I believe he saw his dad when he said, 'Dad is calling me!' I believe he could hear his father calling out. I think the people at the end of the bed were people that he knew although he never said their names. I believe all the people he mentioned were waiting for him. And I believe that I will see Daddy again. That's my personal belief and I think it will happen one day.

ALICE, FROM COUNTY LOUTH, had a visitation from her brother, Kevin, following his death in 2001.

My brother's wife rang me about three weeks before he died and she said he was looking for me. She told me he had said, 'I want to talk to Alice.' That would be highly unusual. We were a close family and always just a phone call away. So I went down to see him. I went straight away.

My brother was very good to everybody else. He was 47. He didn't talk too much or say too much. He wasn't the sort of fellow that ever opened up. But, when we met, we sat and we talked for about three-and-a-half hours. He poured his heart out to me.

He kept saying, 'I'm in this black hole that I can't get out of.' He told me about a lot of the things that were troubling him. He also told me, 'I have a pain in my chest these past three days.' I said, 'You have to go to the doctor.' He said, 'I couldn't go to the doctor.' And he didn't.

We talked and talked. Coming towards the end he kept saying, 'That was the best talk I've ever had with anybody, our lassie.' He always called me 'our lassie' because I'm the only sister in the family and there were lots of boys. I said, 'Why did you leave it to now, Kevin?'

He dropped dead three weeks later, on a Saturday night. The day beforehand he had said to his wife, 'Make me an appointment with the doctor.' But he died before he could see the doctor. He had a massive heart attack. People were trying to resuscitate him. The ambulance came straight away and took him to hospital. But it was too late.

I came home and I went to bed that night. I was having great difficulty getting to sleep. I was lying in my bed and the head of my bed was to the wall. There was a triple wardrobe facing me and a big bay window to the right. There was a bedside locker on either side of the bed. Eventually I must have dropped off.

Sometime during the night my brother was there, right beside me, standing against the left bedside locker. I don't know what woke me, whether I sensed him there or not. But I just opened my eyes and there he was. I was on my left side, facing towards the locker. I got a terrible fright. I couldn't tell you what time it was, even though I had a clock sitting on the locker.

He was there with his legs crossed and he was resting against the edge of the locker. He had his arms folded. He was right beside the bed, about a foot away. He just looked like he always did, with dark blue jeans and a dark brown sweater which had a pattern across the chest. His face was turned towards me.

He said, 'I'm alright now, our lassie!' I could see him as clear as day. He was as real as the day I was talking to him and as clear as if I was looking at somebody now. I'm sure it only lasted seconds. And I don't know whether I then closed my eyes or what. But he just disappeared and was gone. When I opened my eyes again he wasn't there anymore.

It took me ages to get to sleep again. I was restless. I wasn't really frightened although I did get a shock. I had always believed this sort of thing was possible. My mother had died the year beforehand with a massive heart attack. My father had gone, back in 1987, with a massive heart attack also. I often sensed that they were around. I never saw them but I sometimes felt they were in a room with me. I could feel they were there.

I couldn't get what had happened out of my head around the time of the funeral. As I looked at Kevin laid out I said to myself, 'Well, you are alright now.' I think he came back to let me know that he was alright and that he was happy where he was. He probably knew what I was thinking after our conversation three weeks before. I think he was letting me know that he was OK.

I have thought long and hard about it, since then, and I have asked myself, 'Was it real or was it my imagination? Was it a dream?' But I am certain it wasn't a dream. He was too real-looking. He had a physical shape. The voice was the same. He looked the same. And when he turned his head to look at me it was just the way he'd turn his head if you were talking to him. I felt I could have touched him if I put my hand out.

I don't always know the reasons why these things occur but they do happen. I know I got great consolation from seeing him, knowing that he was alright and being happy about where he was. And, although I never saw him again, I have sometimes sensed that he was near. So, while what happened seems incredible, I say to myself, 'Strange things do occur and they certainly happened with me.'

FRANCESCA, FROM BELFAST, believes she saw her deceased brother, Peter, some weeks after his death.

This story goes back to 1987 when my brother died. He was only 45. It was thought he had an overactive thyroid so he went into hospital for a check-up. He was kept in and they ended up treating him for encephalitis, which is a brain inflammation caused by an infection. Initially he seemed to be getting better. But then he got very low again.

The whole thing was unreal. We didn't really know what was happening. It was all taking place so quickly. He had walked into the hospital but he deteriorated very fast. He died within three weeks. We were told afterwards that it was an inoperable brain tumour. It was all very traumatic. It was just horrendous.

A few weeks after that – maybe a month later – I was doing a school run. It was during the afternoon of a nice, normal day. I had my youngest son in the car. It was about three o'clock in the afternoon and we were driving down the Newtownards Road towards traffic-lights, to go back home again.

There was reasonably heavy traffic, with two lanes on each side. I was in the inner lane because I was approaching the traffic-lights and I wanted to turn right. Suddenly I saw my brother passing me on the other side of the road. He was driving and coming towards me. He was right alongside me, in the near lane. We were side by side.

I didn't notice his car, only Peter. He was facing me. I saw the whole front of his face, not just the shape of the back of his head or anything like that. I knew him straight away. He had the pale complexion, the black hair, the narrow face, the pointy nose, the family look. Although he smoked a pipe he wasn't smoking one at that time. It was definitely Peter passing by. I thought, 'Oh, my God!'

He took a while to pass me because the traffic was quite heavy. He was all alone in the car and he never looked at me. I had to calm myself down. It was definitely him. I was positive. I wanted to stop. I wanted to turn the car around. The whole thing might have been only seconds but in my head it was all going in slow motion.

Initially I thought, 'We have made a mistake. He hasn't died. He is still with us. He is still alive. He is on his way back to work.' Then, of course, I thought, 'No. It's not that.' Instead I thought, 'He has come back to me. He is letting me know he is alright.'

I was so relieved that he was alright. I felt comfortable knowing that he was in a happy place, in heaven and aware of us. I thought, 'He is still with us and we are all still together.

He is still very much part of us.' It also made the world seem much smaller and all of us much closer. It was a huge sense of relief at the time.

I don't know why it happened. It was, after all, a month or so after he had died and I shouldn't have been thinking of him at that particular time. I was on a school run, with other things on my mind. Maybe he came to me because we were close. Maybe I was just more sensitive to things like this. Or maybe I was just lucky enough to see him. I don't really know why.

I didn't say it to my mother or father. In fact, although I was so convinced of what had happened, I didn't say it to anyone. But I definitely saw him. He definitely passed me. And it was an experience that definitely happened. I can still visualise it. I can still see the whole thing. It still comes to me once in a while. And I certainly wasn't expecting anything like it on that particular day.

MÁIRÉAD, FROM LIMERICK, recalls how she was visited by her deceased father while out for an early evening walk. Her sister-in-law was battling terminal cancer at the time.

Most evenings my friend and I used to go for a walk up the Plassey bank on the River Shannon. We would go up to the college and back, after supper. One evening, back in 1996, we were walking up the bank. It got a bit dreary and there weren't many people on it. It got a bit darkish. It wasn't night-time but it was a bit dull. It was in May.

At the time my sister-in-law, who lived in England, was dying and I wouldn't accept it. She was only 44 and was given eight weeks to live. She had cancer in her ovaries. I couldn't accept it because she was home a couple of months before and she looked ever so well.

That evening we were nearly onto the Dublin road, where

the rugby pitch is. It was around eight or half-eight. Suddenly this man was walking towards us. He was away back. He was very erect and really clean-looking. He had three little dogs coming along with him. He was walking very erect with the three dogs. It was the walk and the dogs. I knew the walk. I immediately knew it was my father, who had died in 1982.

He looked really well. He looked very fresh. He had the same build. And although my father would never have worn white socks like the man did, and had only one dog and not three, I knew it was him.

He was also much younger than my father would have been when he died, with a younger face. It was like when he was maybe 50 years old, about 40 years younger than when he passed away. He had grey hair but my father was grey when he was young too.

My father, for almost all of his life, had great health. He was always a good worker. He worked very hard. If he had lived another 10 or 12 days he would have been 90 years old. And he had wonderful health up to the last three months. But, when I saw him, the years seemed to have gone back to about 50.

As he came nearer I just started running and I said to my friend, 'This is my father!' She said to me, 'But your father is dead!' I started running towards him but then something stopped me. I waited for my friend and she caught up with me. I said, 'I know he's dead but this is him!'

My father had a special salute for his cousins or his family or his close friends, where he would just wink an eye and smile. It was a nice friendly smile and he had a way of shaking his head when he was doing it. I knew it was his smile. But it was the salute more than anything. I was definite.

At this stage my friend was right by my side. She was on the outer side of me, nearer to him. Yet he didn't look at her at all. He just smiled and saluted at me. It was as if he didn't see her. She later maintained that he didn't see her at all, that it was definitely only special for me.

He walked on slowly. He started looking back and I was looking back at him. He then went up to a gate. He just bent over the gate as if he was looking at cows going away after being milked, like my father used to do when we were at home. After that he bent down to pat the dogs, as my father would do, and he was looking back at us again.

I was struck dumb. I did not know how to deal with it. I wanted so much to speak to him but there were no words. No words were spoken. I said to my friend, 'What will I do?' She didn't know what to say. Inside me my intuition was telling me, 'Stay here.' And that's what I did. But I always think it was a missed opportunity. I should have gone up and spoken to him but somehow I couldn't.

I left him looking back at us and patting the dogs. The two of us walked on, to go home. I never looked back again. And that was it. I said, 'I really wasted the moment. I should have gone up and said hello.' But I didn't and I feel very sad about it now. I am raging that I didn't do a bit more. My friend said I did the right thing. But I should have done something.

My sister-in-law died nine days afterwards. She died in a hospital in England. My brother was with her at the time. He said he needed to go to the toilet for a second. She said, 'You can. You can go now while the room is full of people.' My brother said there was nobody in the room. He went to the toilet and she died in the split second before he came back. It was people coming for her.

What happened on that walk back in 1996 is a strange story. It did happen. And when I look back at it now, I know it was so real. My father's body was so real. Everything he was on earth before he went was there. It was a big thing for me. I think he had come to tell me that he was coming to collect my sister-in-law. I think he was saying, 'Everything is lovely here. I'm coming to collect her and she is coming with me.'

I never saw him again even though I did the walk for a good while after that, over the years. I had never seen him before that day either. It's strange. But I think there are lots of things out there. And there's more than us around here, without a shadow of a doubt.

PHIL, FROM COUNTY CORK, recollects a somewhat different type of vision – this one involving a visit from her deceased father at a time when she was faced with a crisis in her life. The vision, in other words, falls into the 'helpful' category.

I have two lads with special needs. One of them was born with slight brain damage. Doctors were dismissing me, saying it was my imagination. When he was six I brought him to what was the Cork Polio Clinic at the time. I brought him for a check-up. They said, 'Your child is brain damaged. He needs to go to a special school in Cork city.'

I was terribly upset. I thought they were taking him off me. No one explained anything. I was crying every night at the thought of my child going away. I thought I wouldn't see him anymore. We thought he'd be going away and that would be it. No one explained that he would be coming home every weekend. We didn't know what to do.

I was in bed one night when I got a very strong smell of pipe tobacco. My father used to smoke a pipe and I used love the smell from it. Yet he was never in my bedroom in my life. The smell was very strong and it woke me up. I sat up.

I could see my father at the end of the bed, just as he was before he died. He was a fine, good-looking man, nearly six feet tall. He had the pipe in his hand. He was smiling. All he said to me was, 'Let the lad go. He'll be fine. He'll be alright.' That's what my father used always say – 'Everything's going to be alright.'

I could see him perfectly. He was standing straight down in front of me, at the end of the bed. He was dressed in a topcoat and a cap. He was holding the pipe in his right hand, as he always did. But you couldn't see the glow of the pipe. Instead you could just smell it.

He was looking very happy. It was like he was getting ready to go out for a few pints. It all lasted just a couple of minutes. When I got up the following morning I said to my husband, 'We'll go up to the school. We'll take him up.'

It was lovely because I needed someone to tell me what to do. The doctors couldn't tell me because they didn't know anything about the school at the time. At the end of the day, what happened was the best decision possible for the child. It was great. He really learned so much there, including about computers, and he was so happy.

The next time I went down to the doctor I told him what had happened. He looked at me and said, 'Were you close to your father?' I said, 'We were the best of buddies.' He said, 'That was great there was someone who was able to help you.' He was nice about it although I'd say he thought I was going a bit cuckoo.

I took a long while to say it to one of the priests because I thought they would believe I was cracking up. Eventually I said it to one of them. He said, 'If you have enough faith in your parents, and you ask for help when you really need it, they'll come back to you.' I think the priest accepted it while the doctor thought I was cracked.

I never saw my father again although the smell of his pipe lingered in my bedroom for a couple of weeks. But I'm sure he helped me that time. He was that sort of person. He was always there. If you weren't well at home, he was always the first up with a hot cup of tea. He was a great man.

I always say now that people who have problems should talk to those who have died. Some people think that's crazy but I don't. I believe people come back if we talk to them and if we really believe. Some people say they believe but they don't. They laugh at it. But I really believe there's a presence out there, helping us. These things do happen.

TOM BRENNAN, WHO COMES ORIGINALLY FROM COUNTY KILKENNY **but who lives in County Cork, also describes a visitation where help was provided.**

My mother died in 1980, when she was very young, at the age of 47. She was both bulimic and anorexic before it was fashionable to be so. She was gaunt. My father continued to live in County Kilkenny, just outside Castlecomer, but I was living down in Cork. I would go up to visit whenever I could.

One night back in 1983 – a Tuesday night into Wednesday morning – I woke up in the early hours and my mother, who was dead three years, was standing beside the bed. It was probably around three o'clock in the morning. It was just a figure in the shadows, as if a hall light was on and somebody came into the room. She was standing on the right-hand side, about halfway down the bed.

She always called me Thomas. 'Thomas!' she said. 'You'd want to go to Kilkenny! There's something wrong! You're needed up there!' I knew the voice immediately. It wasn't a case that I could see her face or her hands but I knew it was her from the way she spoke to me. That was all she said. I said, 'OK, Mam,' and I just went back to sleep.

I woke up the next morning – the Wednesday morning – and I said, 'My God! That was a weird dream I had last night.' I really thought I had been dreaming but I just couldn't

126

let it go. I felt, 'There's something wrong. I had better get to Kilkenny. My mother told me to go.'

So I got up and belted off to Kilkenny with my wife Anne and my three young daughters. I arrived and my dad, who was then in his early 60s, was there. I asked him, 'Is there something wrong?' and he said, 'No, everything is grand, everything is OK.'

I pottered around for a while and at about three o'clock in the afternoon I said, 'I think I'll go home to Cork.' I got into the car, reversed out of the yard, went into the little boreen and drove up to the T-junction. I would normally turn left to go into Castlecomer and go home, back to Cork. For some reason I couldn't get myself to turn left. Instead I went right, which brought me back up in front of the house.

There was a small field separating me from the house. Dad was at the door with my brother and sister, who were twins. They were waving goodbye. But there was like a blue – a dull blue – fluorescent light around my father. That's the only way I could describe it. I stopped the car and said to Anne, 'Did you see that? Am I seeing things? Is there a light around my father? It's strange.' She said, 'I see nothing.'

I reversed the car and I went back down into the yard by the house. My dad said, 'Did you forget something?' I said, 'No. I didn't. I decided I'm going to stay for the night.' He said, 'You're worse than your mother. You just don't know where you want to be.'

That evening, around eight o'clock, I asked him, 'Would you like to go down for a pint?' My father would drink beer out of an old boot. But he said, 'No. No. I don't want to go down there tonight.' I said, 'OK.' So about ten o'clock I went to bed.

At four o'clock in the morning my sister, who was one of the twins, came running into the room. She said, 'Tom! Tom!

Get up quick! Dad is not well!' I got up and saw him leaning on the window-sill and the muscles in his back were actually shivering. I got him over to the doctor, who gave him an injection. He was having a massive heart attack.

The doctor said, 'I'm calling an ambulance. Stay with your dad because I don't expect him to live to see the ambulance.' I stayed with him, rubbing his arm and his chest. I was saying, 'It's alright, Dad. The ambulance is on its way.' Eventually the ambulance arrived and took him away.

I stayed with him for two days and then came back to Cork, to work. There was a Guard where I live and in the middle of the following week – a Wednesday night – he came up and banged on my door. 'Tom,' he said, 'you'd want to get to Kilkenny fast. Your dad is not expected to live the night.' I had no diesel in my car at the time and another man actually came, at 12 o'clock on a Wednesday night, to fill my car. I bombed it up to Kilkenny.

When I got to the hospital I was walking down to where my dad was and the nurse tried to stop me. I asked her, 'Is my dad still alive?' She said, 'Yes.' I said, 'I want to see him.' She brought me in and pulled back the curtains. And Dad was there in the bed, as blue – that dull blue – as the colour I saw the week before.

I asked the nurse, 'What's wrong with him?' She rolled him over and she showed me where they stabbed him right into the heart with adrenaline. She said, 'We gave him so much electricity it turned his dermis blue. It happens.' It was unreal. It was frightening to see it. But he lived for about ten or twelve years after that and he eventually died of cancer.

I just cannot explain what happened. It's amazing. I often ponder on it. I'm convinced my mother came back to me. I've told people several times, 'I don't care what you say. If she didn't tell me and I didn't go to Kilkenny, my dad would be dead.'

There are things we cannot explain. We are more complex and there is something greater to us than we give ourselves credit for. We are something special, something extraordinary. It's just one of those things. But I'm absolutely positive my mother came to me. I believe it in my heart and soul. She was real and vivid that night. She just said those few words and she was gone.

RICHARD T. COOKE, FROM COUNTY CORK, **was visited by a comforting face at three critical, and near-fatal, moments in his life.**

I grew up in a lovely area in Cork city called the North Mall. I was like Huckleberry Finn, living there, because alongside it was the glorious River Lee. It could have been the Mississippi. My pastime was around the river, down the old slip, fishing and playing around on summer days. I swam in the river and played in the river and had a passion for it. There was always something to do but, above all, we always had a passion for fishing.

One evening I ventured off on my own – which I usually used to do – and I was waiting until the lads came down. It was a windy old night. We used to fish from on top of St. Vincent's Bridge. There used to be balls of eels around the pillars that held up the bridge and there would be various fish coming and going. I was up on top of the bridge. There must have been a gust of wind and I fell off the bridge into the river. Off I went into the Lee.

I was probably 500, 600 or 700 yards away from the slip. That was a long distance and the water was moving fast. It was a pretty high tide and it was fast-flowing. I was able to swim but I wasn't good enough to get myself back onto land.

I had only learned to swim by myself after falling in at the old slip. So I was underneath the water.

Suddenly I saw a face. This beautiful face appeared to me. It was underneath with me. I can still see it in my own mind's eye today. It was a smiling face, with a lovely warm glow. It was a young, happy, bright, friendly face. Even up to today I wouldn't know if it was a male or a female but it was absolutely beautiful.

I must have lost consciousness and I woke up on the slip, 500, 600 or 700 yards away. I was actually sitting on one of the steps. There was only one slip on the whole North Mall and I ended up sitting on one of the steps there. I just don't know how it happened. I really don't know how I got there.

There was nobody around to help me and it would have been impossible for me to pull myself out of the water whose current was dragging me down. I still don't understand what happened. Something from the other side must have picked me up and put me there.

About nine years afterwards I was down in a dancehall in Blackrock. Myself and two friends were absolutely sweating so we left the dancehall and we went down onto the small stone strand that was there. We decided to go out in an old punt. The three of us went out. We were talking about the dance and so on.

One of my friends was a big, handsome-looking guy. He started dancing in the punt and all of a sudden it went over. I was wearing brown boots at the time, which were in the fashion of the era, and a lot of gear. I began to sink. I was being dragged down, pulled down like a big stone. I was panicking. And panic kills.

Once again I saw that face. It was exactly the same face, with the same smile. I became more calm and in control of my senses. It gave me a conscious awareness to take off my boots.

I untied my boots and took off my coat. If I didn't I wouldn't be alive now.

I came back up to the top of the water and was looking for the other two. I found them and we made it back onto the strand. We were brought up to the South Infirmary and we were fine. That was when I was around 18 years of age, eight or nine years after I first saw the face.

I saw the same face for a third time as well. There was a programme came on RTÉ for young musicians and young composers. I was invited to go on it. I was doing my recording and I felt nauseous and very ill. I was taken to hospital and they found that my appendix had burst. I was out for a few days and I was told if I was half an hour later I would have been dead. That's when I saw that face again. But this time it was in a tunnel of white light. You could see the face within the beautiful light. That was three times and I haven't had the experience since.

Looking back, I believe somebody was looking after me. I think people who die are still part of us. They have not gone away. Their spirit is alive. I believe we all have a path and I don't believe in coincidence at all. I believe things happen for a reason and we have to learn from them or grow from them. And I absolutely believe that people come back from the other side.

In my own instance, I don't know why I was specifically picked out. Other people have drowned. I don't know why I ended up on the slip or untied my bootlaces. But I know that what I saw wasn't an illusion. If it was an illusion I'd be dead.

I still ask, 'Did I see the face in a book? Did I see it in a church?' The truth is I never saw that face anywhere else. I tried to paint it, or draw it, but it never came out right. You just couldn't paint it. But I certainly still remember it to this day and the events have lived on in my mind. And if I am ever feeling anyway off now, all I have to do is think of that face and I feel good.

PHIL, FROM COUNTY CORK, felt the presence of her dead brother while she was experiencing serious problems with her heart.

I had a massive heart attack, about seven years ago, at half-four in the morning. I can remember it like it happened only yesterday. I got a very bad turn in my stomach, as if I ate something that disagreed with me. Then my jawbone started aching, like someone had hit me with a hammer. A couple of minutes after that I got this burning in my back, just above my shoulder-blades. It was like someone had thrown boiled water at me.

I shot up in bed and I screeched. It was in the middle of the dark. My husband got a terrible fright, wondering what was wrong. I said, 'There's something gone wrong inside!' That's exactly the way I described it. I was groggy and frightened. I felt dreadful. I just sat up in bed for the rest of the morning. Something told me to keep sitting up. When I got out of bed I couldn't keep my balance. Eventually my daughter got me down to the doctor.

By that stage my breast was just jumping. It was like the heart was jumping out of me. It was like that when I got up although there was no pain. When I got there the doctor put me on a machine and she called the ambulance straight away. She said nothing to me. She just spoke to my daughter and said, 'She's very bad.'

I got in the ambulance and I was lying on the stretcher. I was on oxygen and felt miserable. I suddenly felt a sort of downwards pressure in the ambulance, as if someone stepped in. I said to the ambulance man, 'I'm safe now. My brother is here.' I felt my brother's presence. The ambulance man looked around but I said, 'You can't see him but I can feel him. He's minding me.'

My brother was dead 21 years at that stage. He had died at 52 from a heart attack. He had been at work in the morning and came home complaining of a pain in his chest. He said he'd go and lie down for a while. He wasn't one for doctors. But his wife found him dead at three o'clock. We had been very close.

When I was in the ambulance it was like he was there touching me and saying, 'You're alright now. Don't worry. You're going to be fine.' It was like he was holding my right hand and standing beside me. I felt very calm and relaxed. Peace washed over me. I had a warm feeling. I knew I was going to be saved.

I couldn't see him or hear him, because he never spoke, but it was like he was standing alongside of me the whole time. I could really feel him. He was like he was when he died. He was with me the whole way to the hospital. And I knew I was going to be alright because he was there to look after me.

When they brought me into Accident and Emergency they put me on a monitor. They discovered I had had a heart attack and had an aneurysm under the breastbone. The doctor turned to my husband and told him to go home and make funeral arrangements. He said, 'She's dying. She's not going to come out of this. She has the most diseased heart we have ever seen.'

They eventually operated on me. I had a bypass and I had my stomach opened as well, to get at the aneurysm. I had arteries taken from my leg. When I was going down to surgery my husband was let in to say goodbye. But I said, 'I'm not saying goodbye because I'm coming out of this. I'm going to be fine.' The doctor said, 'Do you realise how bad you are?

There's an aneurysm there. If that bursts you're gone.' I said, 'It's not going to burst.' I could still feel my brother with me.

I felt he was with me the whole time in the hospital. I felt he was holding my hand as I was going into surgery. I knew he was protecting me. There were times, when there was no one around, that I felt someone rubbing my hair. I often felt it when I was lying in the bed. But there was no one else there and I'm sure it was my brother.

Eventually I was discharged from the hospital. I had to go back for a check-up after two weeks and the surgeon was there to meet me. He jokingly said, 'Get out of my office, you're dead! There's no way you should be walking around!' He had said I was either going to die or have a massive stroke. I actually said to the surgeon, 'Someone above loves me.' He wasn't happy with that. He kind of got snappy and said, 'There's no one above. We're down here.' But I believe my brother is down here all the time, watching me.

There's definitely someone minding us. I firmly believe that. I said it to our priest, who came up to see me every day. He said, 'You have better faith than I have. The Almighty God is working through your brother for you.' I felt very reassured by that.

I still think of my brother all the time, even now. If I have a problem at home I still talk to him. I feel peaceful and reassured and know I'm going to be looked after. I know he's above looking down at me. He's the brightest star in the sky.

I also talk to my mother and father. I had a brother-in-law who died suddenly too. I talk to them all. When I go to visit them in the graveyard I know there's nothing in the ground. But their presence is still there. It's there all the time and they walk with us.

HUGH FLYNN, WHO COMES FROM COUNTY LONGFORD **but who now lives in County Cork, describes what occurred when he came perilously close to drowning.**

It happened back in the 1950s, when I was only 19 or 20 years old. I was in the Defence Forces at the time and living in Mullingar. One evening four of us, who were dressed in our army uniforms, decided to go for a walk. We went to a bridge on the canal. We were just sitting there and enjoying ourselves when someone had a bright idea.

One of the fellows said, 'I wonder who'd be brave enough to swim across that water with a cigarette in his mouth for two shillings?' I couldn't really swim at the time but I decided to have a go. I took my uniform off and stripped down to my underwear. I put a cigarette in my mouth. In I went, heading off across the water, trying to swim with the cigarette in my mouth while not getting it wet.

I never made it across. The currents were so strong that I was dragged down into the water. I saw weeds or debris or whatever in front of me. I went into a terrible panic. I realised I was in trouble. I came up again to the top of the water. I could see the lads about four metres away and I shouted. I sank again. I was really in trouble. I came up once more and shouted. And then I sank for a third time.

It was then that I saw the figure of Our Lord. He was dressed in white. His hands were down by his side, slightly away from him. He was very clear and was looking at me. He had a beautiful facial expression although he wasn't saying anything. He also had long hair. I can still see him and I can still see his hair.

He kept looking at me and I kept looking at him. I kept saying to him, 'I'm coming to you! I'm coming to you!' I suppose at that stage I was doing exactly that – coming to him. I was so happy. I felt happy because I was going to him. The way that I felt is still as clear to me today as it was all those years ago.

People might say it could have been mind over matter. It could have been some type of hallucination. I don't know. But I don't believe so. He was absolutely clear to me, straight in front of me. He was standing there, looking at me. It was so real. I still believe it could have been nobody else but Christ.

The next thing I was on the canal bank. It seems that one of my army friends jumped into the water, fully clothed. He had his army boots on and his money in his pockets. He got hold of me and brought me over to the other bank. The other lads pulled me onto the bank. One of them pumped water out of me. A doctor was called and they got an ambulance and I was taken away. They took me to hospital and linked me up to all sorts of tubes.

They let me out about two or three hours afterwards. It seems strange now but I made straight away for the fields. I started touching the grass and the trees and the bushes and the cows. I honestly believed that I wasn't alive. I thought I was dead. I felt I had gone somewhere. That lasted for about four or five days.

I often wondered about what happened. I wondered had it something to do with my grandfather. I had lived with him since I was very young. He had been blinded in the 1914 – 1918 war. I used to lead him around. I was his sight. I would bring him to mass. People used to call me 'the little boy who led the blind man around.' Maybe I was being rewarded for that.

Maybe Our Lord led my army colleague to save my life. I still have a photograph in my house of that man. He was a lovely lad. Strangely, for the rest of our time in the army we never spoke. I don't know why. He just kept his distance from me. I think he felt that I might feel under obligation to him for saving my life. Maybe that's why.

Either way, the event left an impact on me. The vision of what I believe was Christ has lived with me all down through the years. I got great strength from it. I go to church. I think about what happened at times when I am in trouble. And, when I look back, I believe I was dying and in the presence of Christ. A few moments later and I would have been dead.

KATHLEEN HEALY, FROM COUNTY WICKLOW, recalls how her mother, Maisie, had a strange experience shortly before she passed away. What occurred belongs to the death-bed vision category.

Cigarettes killed my mother. She loved them. She was smoking since she was 16. She had emphysema as a result. She had a wheeze and her chest was in a bad way. It all caught up with her. She used to go in and out of the hospital and the doctor used to say to her, 'You will live longer if you give up those cigarettes.'

The last time I went in to collect her, to bring her home, I was with her when she saw the doctor before she was released. It was so funny. He used to call her by her first name. He said to her, 'Maisie, do you have a packet of cigarettes with you?' She didn't realise that what he was trying to say was that cigarettes make you very ill, do a lot of damage and cause death. She thought he was asking for one. She said, 'Why, would you like one?' She was being kind. He said, 'I give up.'

We were worried about her. She was 75 at the time and her breathing wasn't great. My father, Michael, had died about a year and seven months prior to that. So she was at home in the house by herself. Her son, Gerard, who lived with her, was away on holiday at the time. As a result, my daughters took turns going down to look after her and stay with her. I would go down to her all the time too.

I was down with her on the following Saturday night. I was changing covers and putting up clean curtains and doing everything. She didn't have the energy to do them. I remember she was up in bed, in the same room that she and Daddy had always slept in. I went up to her and she said, 'Get in there and lie down beside me, you're exhausted.' I fell asleep and didn't wake up until five o'clock in the morning.

The moment I woke up I saw her beside me, sitting up in the bed with the pillow behind her. She was awake. She had probably been awake all the time. She said to me, 'Your father is after coming for me!' I just looked at her. My mother was very with it. There wasn't anything wrong with her mind. She was on the ball about everything. I said, 'Are you after being asleep?' She said, 'No, but it's time for me to be going.'

I said, 'Where would you be going?' She repeated, 'Your daddy came to me and he was at the end of the bed!' She pointed down to where he had been. She said, 'He smiled at me and I'll be joining him shortly because it's time for me to go.' I looked at her and said, 'Don't be ridiculous.' She said, 'No. I'm not being ridiculous. I'll not be here much longer. I'll be joining him shortly. I'll be going home.'

She smiled at me as she said it and looked happy. I thought it was very strange. I couldn't understand what she meant. I must have been in some sort of shock. But her words stayed with me. And what she said played on my mind the next day.

That next day was a Sunday and my daughter, Róisín, was staying over with her. She would have only been about 13 and she brought her school uniform with her because she would have gone off directly to school on the Monday. My mother got bad with her breathing and Róisín knew she wasn't good. She rang for the ambulance. They came and Mammy went off to the hospital. I never knew anything about this until the next day.

It was then that I told my husband, Brendan, what she had said. He said, 'That's not like Maisie.' He knew she was very with it. Some people might say strange things or repeat themselves as they get older but not her – she was always bang on. I also thought about it myself and I knew that what she said was very unusual.

It wasn't that it was unusual for her to talk about my father. They had been very close. I remember going up to their bedroom one morning when they were both alive. It was early, about a quarter-to-eight, before the children would have gone to school. The two of them were asleep, my mother in my father's arms, like two little lovebirds. I thought it was the loveliest thing I had ever seen.

That stayed with me. But, while she was very close to my father and told stories about the times when he was alive, she had never said anything like him being 'at the end of the bed.' So I wondered about it. But I said to myself that she was looking too well and I kind of put it at the back of my mind. I said, 'No, she'll be coming back home again.'

Around the middle of the next week she was still in the hospital and she looked fine. She was in great form, talking and laughing. But, for whatever reason, I rang my brother, Dominic, in England and he said, 'That doesn't sound good. I'm going to come home.' Something must have clicked with me to ring him because I hadn't rung him before. He came home on the Thursday and she died on the Saturday morning, a week after she said she saw my father at the end of the bed.

I firmly believe that my father did come to my mother near the end. My mother wasn't the type of person to just say things like that for the sake of saying them. She wouldn't have invented it. She would never tell a lie. We were all brought up to never tell lies. He would have been there, looking at her.

They were so united that he would definitely have come when it was time for her to go. They were so close and they got on so well that that would certainly have happened. So I definitely believe it did occur. And I believe my mother and father are together now in heaven and are once again happy. She has definitely 'gone home' to my daddy.

JAN, FROM COUNTY DONEGAL, describes her mother's death-bed visions in the months before she passed away.

The first event happened in 1997, about ten months before my mother died. She was staying with me at the time. I was looking after her. Although she was 100 years old, she was very alert. She was a quiet, reserved person. She loved reading romantic novels. She was very mobile and could do things on her own. She could feed herself, dress herself and all that. But she stayed inside the house and she didn't go out much. She was an astonishing woman.

One day she was sitting in a chair, looking out the window into the garden. She suddenly said to me, 'Who is the man in the garden?' I looked out and I saw nobody. I said to her, 'There isn't anybody there.' She said, 'There is! There's a man in the garden and he is looking in at me!' I went and looked outside in case I had missed something.

The garden had a lawn and shrubs and bushes. It's a quiet garden, with tall trees. I looked around it but there was nobody there. I thought, for a while, that maybe my husband had passed by and I had missed him. I thought that's who she had seen. But it wasn't my husband. So I came back in again and I said, 'I don't see anybody.'

She said, 'Look out again! The man is looking in at me and he is smiling!' I asked her, 'Who does he look like and what is he wearing?' She described the man in detail. She said he had a mop of white hair and he was wearing a dark suit and a white shirt and a blue tie. It was a vivid picture of my father. That's exactly the way he dressed, going out on an occasion. It was just like him.

She didn't, however, associate what she saw with her late husband. He had died 38 years earlier. He had only been 62 when he died. By this stage she had kind of forgotten him. If I spoke about him she would ask, 'Who was he? What was he like?' I think the picture of him had faded in her mind. It was a combination of her getting old and it being a long time since she was with him.

At the time I didn't know what to make of what happened. I thought about it as time went on. It was quite clear to me that it was my father she was describing. I believe she saw a vision of him and I still believe it to this day. I also had a vague feeling that maybe death was on its way. She certainly was smiling all the time she saw him and then she lay back on the chair and fell asleep. When she woke up again she didn't mention it anymore and neither did I.

The second event happened at the start of the following year, 1998. She died that January of old age. She was almost 101. It happened shortly before she died. She was in bed all the time at that stage. She was still reading – her last book being a prayer book. We had converted a small room off the kitchen into a bedroom for her. That was for convenience for both her and for me. I could keep an eye on her when I was in the kitchen working about.

One Saturday morning, at 11 o'clock, I was sitting on the edge of the bed giving her a cup of tea. She had a pale blue knitted bed jacket on. Her hair was beautiful. She always liked her hair to be in good shape. She had lovely wavy hair. It was all combed back. I always liked to do it. She was looking very well, propped up on the pillows, looking out. I had her propped up so that she could see out into the kitchen, where I was working.

Suddenly this beautiful smile came over her face. It was as if her whole face lit up. Her eyes were wide open and as blue as blue could be. She said to me, 'There's your dad!' She put one arm out and her hand was wide open, like she was reaching for somebody. I thought she was stretching out for the cup, which I didn't give her.

I turned around and there was nobody there. I turned back again and she said to me, 'Did you see him?' I said, 'Yes.' I couldn't say anything else at that time. She then said to me, 'Isn't he looking good?' I said, 'Yes, he is.' That was the full conversation we had. But it was the smile on her face that really caught my attention. It was as if her face was glowing. And I clearly remember that her big wide-open eyes were as blue as could be.

Then, after she had her cup of tea, she lay back on her pillows and she fell asleep. Again I thought that the end was coming near. At this stage I knew she was fading. I knew she was getting weaker and she wasn't eating anything. She was just taking sips of tea. I didn't know when it would happen but I found out soon enough. She didn't wake up the following day. In fact, she never woke up again. She died on the following Monday evening, at six o'clock.

I believe that she saw my father. I have absolutely no doubt in my mind. Even after all these years, it has stayed vividly with me. I still see it quite clearly. I never thought deeply about it but I do believe there is something beyond life. I think there has to be, especially after experiencing something like that, where my father came back to welcome my mother. I believe she definitely saw somebody. And it certainly was a lovely experience.

MARIE, FROM COUNTY WATERFORD, recollects what took place at the death-bed of her mother, who died in 1998 at the age of 90. Her mother's name was Mae.

My mother had been very lively all her life and had reared a big family but she had been getting old. For about five years we had been minding her at home. Eventually she developed Alzheimer's. She needed hospital care. So for the last four years of her life she was in the local hospital.

She settled in very well. She was a great patient and they looked after her. They were brilliant with her and with everybody else too. She enjoyed her four years in there. Eventually, however, she started to go downhill. We had been told by the hospital that she was low and we spent most of our time with her. I used to visit her every day.

Within a week or so before she became very ill she said to me several times, 'Daddy has come to me! He was here today!' By that she meant her husband, my father, who had died a long time earlier. Or she would say, 'Nan was here!' That's what we used to call her mother, who had also passed away.

She would normally say these things when I'd take her for a walk down the corridor. We'd sit down and I'd be talking to her about things that happened during the day. That's when she'd say them. They were lucid remarks, made in her lucid moments. They were always made in the morning time and that's the best time with Alzheimer's.

I knew they weren't something she was making up. I knew she wasn't talking rubbish. She was totally clear. You'd know if she was making them up because she'd have silly talk in with them. It made her so happy and I was happy for her. I knew she believed them and she was certain they happened. I believed every word she told me.

Eventually she became very low. I had a problem around that time because my daughter went into labour. My husband and I were below in the hospital with her, about 30 miles away. We had been below for a day and part of the next day.

The word was coming down from the hospital, from my sisters, 'Mammy is very low. She won't last.' It really upset me so much because I had looked after her for five years before she went into hospital and it was just the one day in my whole life that I couldn't be with her.

Eventually another daughter of mine rang and said, 'She won't go before you are home because I'm after asking her. I got her on my own and I whispered to her to wait. I bet she won't go before you come back.' So we arrived home at eight o'clock in the morning, changed our clothes and went in to be with her.

By that stage she was in this ward on her own. That day there must have been about 30 of us in there too. My sisters and brothers and grandchildren were there. Her sister was there also. We all wanted to be there with her. She had been a great mother and had reared nine of us. Times were hard in those days but everyone who came to the village was welcome. She'd feed them and look after them. She was very good-living. She had great faith. She was liked by everybody. The grandchildren adored her too.

We were all there – her sister holding one hand with me holding her other hand and everyone else standing around – and there was plenty of room. We were all in a circle, sitting there, talking quietly. I was on one side of the bed and her sister was on the other.

The nurses came in and they told us that she would die soon. Her pulse was very low. They just turned her and settled her. She was lying down in the bed, looking very peaceful. She hadn't moved for two days. She hadn't spoken for at least that time either.

All of a sudden my mother sat straight up in the bed. Her two eyes opened wide. They were huge, just like big saucers. She was looking straight ahead of her, slightly up a bit but not focused on anybody. She was gazing ahead at this wonder. She had this look on her face. And she had a big smile. It's indescribable.

No one enticed her to sit up. Nobody helped her. She sat up of her own accord. I still had her hand caught and so had her sister. But we weren't supporting her. The wonder on her face was unbelievable. It was some experience. After about 20 seconds she just fell back and she was gone. She died at around one o'clock and I really think she had waited for me.

We all saw it. We were all astounded. Everyone stood and gasped. We all knew straight away that somebody had come to meet her. It was obvious. Her sister shouted, 'What's wrong with Mae? What's wrong with Mae?' Her daughter-in-law said, 'It's alright. Mae is going to heaven.' Her sister replied, 'I'll never be afraid to die now.'

I am very proud to have been there and I will never forget the wonder on her face as she was dying. I will never forget her eyes wide open in astonishment. And I would love to know who came to meet her. It was probably Daddy or her mother, or both, because they were the people she had been speaking about for a few days.

I would never be afraid to die after it. Before, at the thought of dying, I'd panic. But now I wouldn't. I know that I'll be going somewhere. I always had a belief about life after death but that proved it for me. I know there's more to it than just dying. I also know that people come back. And I know I will meet my mother and other relatives again someday.

DESSIE HYNES, WHO COMES FROM COUNTY LONGFORD but who now lives in County Wexford, remembers how a close friend, prior to his death, was visited by a deceased mutual acquaintance.

There was a group of us who were friends and who were very close to each other ever since the late 1940s or early 1950s. There were up to 12 of us altogether. We all knew each other well. We were people who could talk to one another. Nobody would ever be stuck for a pound or five shillings if they were part of the group.

One was a fellow named Jim. He came from a gas family and he was a wonderful character. He was 23 years a medical student. When he qualified he became the registrar in a hospital for another 23 years. Then he retired. After that he walked the canal with a brother-in-law of mine and then dropped dead.

There was another person in the group, called Mattie. He was also a medical student for a time. He did second med. He was a very good friend of Jim's and a friend to all of us as well. He was very bright but he didn't qualify as a doctor. Instead his father had left him a few bob. Then he qualified for social welfare. He wasn't well off.

Mattie had a flat in the Dublin suburb of Rathmines. It was a flat of the 1950s. He used to call it a 'dungeon'. It was a basement flat, two steps down. I used to call in there a lot. Anytime I'd pass by I'd go in and out. He used to smoke a lot. His lungs were gone and he couldn't breathe. He was really in a bad way with emphysema.

About two or three years after Jim had died, I was up there one day to see Mattie. When I went in he said, 'I'm gone!' I said, 'What are you talking about?' He said, 'You won't be seeing me much longer. I won't be here. I'll be going.' I said,

'What?' He said, 'Last night, sometime around four or five o'clock in the morning, I woke up and Jim was at the end of the bed. He came looking for me.'

He went on to explain, 'It didn't look like the end of the bed. There were pillars there just like in Longford Cathedral or in the White House. They were those sorts of big stone pillars. In the middle of them was an opening. And there was Jim in the middle and he was waving me in.

'There was no sound or anything. I just saw Jim's two hands waving me in. I'll be going soon. I won't be around much longer. You might see me once more but that will be it.' To me, I could see the big pillars and Jim waving. I could visualise it in my own mind.

Mattie was dead within a week, maybe four or five days. I was phoned by a guy named Gallagher, who used to fix televisions and he lived near Mattie. He was very good to him. He would get milk and different things for him and leave them on the window-sill. He was a great man, from Donegal, a very kind man.

One day he went down with the milk and he found that Mattie wasn't well. He got an ambulance. Then he phoned me to say that Mattie had gone into the hospital and that he wouldn't be around long. Mattie hardly got to the hospital. I never saw him alive after that. He was dead within a couple of hours. He died aged 71 or 72.

I wasn't in the least bit surprised. I had granduncles and other relatives who would talk about things like this. I would listen to them when I was young. They firmly believed that you never left this world. The spirit, or something, stayed behind. They believed that you could brush against something or be sitting down in a chair and be beside someone else. I had listened to them speaking. So was I surprised? No.

I know Mattie saw Jim. I have no doubt in the world that

he did. He told a few of us what had happened, not just me. He told Gallagher exactly the same thing, 'I'll be leaving soon. Don't be bothered about the milk because Jim is coming for me.' And he wasn't a drinker at the time. He'd just have a few pints and he'd read a lot. So I know he saw it. I have no doubt in the world whatsoever.

YVONNE O'DRISCOLL, FROM DUBLIN, witnessed how her father, John English, was in communion with a greater power shortly before his death from cancer in 2009.

My father became ill back in 2008. He was diagnosed with bladder cancer and was treated quite successfully with radiotherapy at that point. He got a good year at first. I always felt it was a pity that he didn't enjoy this time more. He had great fear and anxiety. Although he had some slight symptoms, none of them were painful. He could have enjoyed this time a lot better.

His illness progressed and by the end of summer 2009 he was complaining of backache. It transpired to be secondary cancer in his spine and he wasn't treatable at that stage except in a palliative care way. The diagnosis was confirmed on a Friday and he then started his palliative care the following Wednesday. On the Thursday evening he developed very high blood pressure and went into renal failure.

His consultant spoke to him and said, 'You're in renal failure.' My father asked, 'Will I die?' The consultant said, 'Yes. You're going to die in the next day or two.' The answer was honest, which is how he had been treated all along the line. Every question he asked was answered honestly but he didn't ask many questions.

He was a practising Catholic. He prayed on a daily basis and went to mass. He continued to practise until he went into hospital that last time. It was never clear how much comfort he got from that. It was never a deep faith, it seemed to me. It was more of a ritual and a reason for getting out of bed in the morning to meet up with a few of the neighbours.

Once he was told he had only a day or two, he became exhausted by the sheer enormity of it all. He had a blood transfusion and a mobile X-ray done in his room. He was hooked into all sorts of things. My brother and I were with him. We said to him, 'Dad, just go to sleep for a while.' His terribly frightened, childlike response was, 'I don't want to go. I must stay awake.' He was very frightened at that stage. He was also quite fitful and distressed.

At one stage he said, 'I don't want to leave you but I have no choice.' A while later he said, 'I'm falling asleep. I'm going now. This is the end of it. I won't see you anymore. Goodbye.' It was very distressing. We thought he might last much longer and we were thinking of palliative care for maybe six months. Suddenly he was dying in front of us.

After a few hours of sleep he woke up and the feebleness and the anxiety and the childhood dependence were all gone. He was very clear and authoritative. He spoke in a very strong, dominant voice and said, 'The Lord said it won't be tonight! You can go home!' He said it with total conviction. He was very clear about it. What he said was very meaningful.

The whole terror and anxiety and fear and dependence were gone. He had passed all that. He was in the care of something better than us. He had moved on. I really feel he had found something that was tranquilising and meaningful. I think he was in communion with heaven. There was no doubt in my mind that he knew what he was talking about. I think it was very significant.

We had been told earlier by the night nurse, 'He's sleeping very deeply. He'll slip away soon. It will be a relief to him.' But this was a dominant, strong voice and he was telling us like he had never told us anything else in his life. I believe something had definitely happened. I don't think that a lot of people would believe it but he was very certain and I received it as that. And I know and believe from my own faith and prayer that this is very possible.

He was a totally different person after that. The nurses were wondering, 'What's going on here?' He was fearless. His organs were switching off but his mind was clear and strong. He was on the mobile phone saying, 'My time is up. You've been a great pal.'

He sat and talked and reminisced with his brother, who came up from Limerick. He got out of bed and walked the corridor. He finally went to bed and he slept. All the agitation and anxiety were gone. His speech went but the pulse was holding up. He eventually drew his last breath on Sunday evening, at six o'clock on the dot.

I can still hear loud and clear what he said that night – 'The Lord said it won't be tonight! You can go home!' It's been on my mind since he died. My mother had gone ahead of him and so had his parents and lots of other people. He had always believed he was going to see them again and I think there were other times he had received messages or directives from deceased loved ones along the line.

But I don't think that he had been communicating with deceased loved ones that night. I don't think it was coming from them. Instead I think that his God told him that night that he was alright, that he needn't be afraid, that he was safe, to stop fighting it, that he was going to a good place, that it was time and he was going home. I absolutely believe that.

STRANGE PREMONITIONS

More than two centuries ago, back in 1808, a Dublin woman by the name of Mrs. Norris had a peculiar dream. In it, her friend Elisa Carleton – who had recently passed away – paid an unexpected visit. The deceased woman reportedly told Mrs. Norris that she would return to inform her of her pending death 24 hours before it occurred.

What happened next was chronicled in the *Proceedings Of The Society For Psychical Research* which was published much later that century – in 1899, to be precise. The journal featured contributions from both Mrs. Norris's son, Thomas James Norris, from Dalkey, County Dublin, and her regular physician, Dr. Richard John Lyon.

The story they told was intriguing. The son described how on 3 March 1864 – 56 years after the dream – his mother, Mrs. Norris, announced that Elisa Carleton had come to her and told her that 'she would die the morning of the next day, at that same hour.' She added that she had just taken a bath so that there would be no necessity for her body to be washed following death.

Although apparently in sound health, she then, as her son put it, 'began to sink, little by little' and died on the day and at the time she had specified. This information was confirmed by the doctor, who was aware of Elisa Carleton's most unusual pact. He wrote: 'The night that preceded her death she announced that the warning for which she had waited fifty-six years had been given her, and that she would die the following night, a thing that happened.'

It seems most strange that anyone should receive such an accurate forewarning of any event not least their own death. However, advance warnings, presentiments and premonitions such as the case above are not uncommon. Indeed, a number of uncannily-accurate predictions of imminent death or near-fatal tragedies are included in the case histories featured in this chapter.

There are many types of premonitions contained in the pages ahead. At times the warnings are delivered by figures appearing in dreams or during nightmares. Other times the warnings are revealed during waking hours. Sometimes they are characterised by an ominous sense of dark foreboding. Occasionally they involve the sound of 'knocking'. Above all, the stories are honestly told by ordinary people whose lives have been forever marked by the events that took place.

MONICA, FROM COUNTY LIMERICK, had a premonition of a near-accident which occurred in 1994. The premonition may have saved her life.

I had two young daughters at the time. One was aged eight and I had a younger daughter who was almost three. The older one had broken her hand and had it in plaster. On one occasion she had an appointment at the Regional Hospital. Although I was a fairly new and nervous driver, I decided that I'd take her to the hospital the following day.

The night before her appointment, I went to bed. It was around eleven o'clock. I woke up, possibly at two or three in the morning, after an awful nightmare. It was so vivid. I could see myself driving out from the hospital. I came to the Roxboro roundabout. As I was exiting the roundabout to my road home, there was a truck in front of me.

The truck was like a council tipper truck although it didn't belong to the council. It was the sort of truck that would transport sand and gravel. It had a red cab and the rest of it was silver. It was right in front of me. All of a sudden, my car wouldn't stop. I could see myself going right under the back of the truck.

I knew we were all going to be killed in seconds. Time seemed to be so limited. I looked across at my daughter in the passenger seat beside me. I looked at my younger daughter directly behind her, in her baby seat. I just didn't want them to realise that they were going to get killed. I didn't want them to be frightened.

I woke up with a start. I snapped out of it. It was just as we were going under the truck. The perspiration was pumping out through me. It was all so real. I got out of bed and thought, 'Oh, God!' I put it down to a nightmare. After a while I got back into bed and fell asleep again.

The same nightmare came to me once more. It was like rewinding a video. I had the very same thoughts. There was the same truck ahead of me. There were the bars on the side of the roundabout, which were a grey metal colour at the time. I had the dream a third time that night, as well, and I was absolutely petrified.

After the third nightmare I got up out of bed and made tea. I then went back to bed again but I couldn't sleep. Suddenly I heard what was like a voice. I couldn't say whether it was a male or female voice. It just came into my head and imprinted itself on my brain. It said, 'Don't drive the car tomorrow!' It was more like a command than a suggestion. After hearing it I lay in bed wondering what I should do.

I spoke to my husband in the morning. I didn't go into exactly what had happened. I just told him I had a bad feeling about driving to the hospital. I told him I was thinking of cancelling the appointment. He said, 'Sure, I'll drive.' And he did. So I forgot about the dream.

After the hospital appointment my husband drove to the Crescent Shopping Centre. We then left for home. I was in the front passenger seat and my two girls were in the back. My husband was driving fairly handily. We were taking a right turn for the road home. Suddenly there was a Volvo in front of us. My husband slammed his leg on the brake. There was no brake. It had completely failed. He said, 'Oh, Jesus!' or something like that.

He had the presence of mind to pull on the handbrake. The car eventually stopped. We didn't hit anything. He narrowly avoided the other car. I was shaking. He got an awful fright. We were both shocked. He said, 'How did you know that something would happen? How did you know the brake was going to fail?' I then told him about the dream.

It was really only after I came home, and we were talking about it, that I realised that if I had been driving I would have gone to the Parkway Shopping Centre to buy my messages. I wouldn't have gone to the Crescent because I was a nervous driver and it was too confusing for me. Therefore, at the time of the crash, I would have already arrived at the Roxboro roundabout. Instead, my husband had taken a detour, which caused a delay. I would have definitely been at the Roxboro. The thought really frightened me.

Every time I now pass the Roxboro roundabout I think of that day. I know that what happened wasn't coincidence. What I saw in my dreams was too vivid. And I just know for a fact that I wouldn't have thought of pulling the handbrake. I know that I would not have been capable of doing that.

I now feel that somehow our lives are mapped out. I know that we were certainly saved from death. I know that somebody up there was looking after me. Whoever it was warned me not to go. Even now, when I drive, I feel certain that I'm going to be fine. And when I pass through the Roxboro roundabout, I feel good because I am so thankful that we were all saved from a terrible fate.

MAUREEN, FROM YORKSHIRE in the UK but who has Irish connections, explains how the details of a dream alerted her to an affair her husband was having.

In the early 1980s I was married and living with my husband and children. My children were young at the time and my husband was working. We were living a normal life. He came home every day at lunch and would have his dinner. I worked in the evenings. I didn't get back until late.

My husband was supposed to be looking after the children although I found out later that it was my eldest son who warmed up the meals and things like that. I suspected he was having an affair. He was popular with the ladies. I always knew he was up to something. I don't know why I knew – I just did. When I would ask him he would deny it.

I started having dreams at one stage. It wasn't unusual for that to happen. Since I was a child I had them. They were normal dreams where you don't remember everything. But these dreams were different. They were a bit like visions. I had them about three or four times. They were all about the same thing, over and over again.

In the dream it was as if I was driving, even though I didn't drive at the time. There was nobody with me. It was daytime. I was going down this road. It was a very long road. The road went around a corner and it turned to the left. There were terraced houses all along the street. They were very dark and dirty-looking on the outside.

Halfway down, on the right-hand side, there was like an

alley through the houses. It was like a break in the houses. By this time I was walking. I looked up and I could see the backs of these houses. I saw coal sheds and outside toilets. Over the top of them I could see the roofs of a row of four or five houses. But I never entered the alley.

Then I woke up. I knew immediately that the dream had something to do with my husband. I just felt it. I challenged him about it. We were in the living-room. I said, 'I had a dream.' He said, 'Yeah?' I asked him, 'Are you seeing somebody else?' He said, 'No.' I then told him what I had seen in my dream. The colour just drained from him. He went like marble.

He was poleaxed, dumbfounded. He was gobsmacked by what I described, the street and the alley and the houses. He couldn't believe it. He said, 'Who told you?' He couldn't understand how I knew. I said, 'Nobody told me. I have seen it.' I must have scared the hell out of him. He then owned up.

He told me he had met a young woman who had a child. He said he felt sorry for her. The affair had gone on for at least a year. He said he was sorry and he would never do it again. He told me, 'I have learned my lesson.' So we stayed together. I couldn't see why his fancy woman should get everything. I also wanted to look after my children and take care of them.

A couple of days later he said, 'I'm going to show you something. Come on. Get in the car.' So we travelled to a place about five miles away. As soon as we turned onto that street I knew it immediately. Halfway down, he stopped the car. We both got out. In front of me was exactly what I had seen in my dreams. It turned out to be where his girlfriend lived. So it was true. And I was right. He said, 'I can't believe it!'

I am really not surprised by what happened. I had dreams before, some of which I hadn't understood and some that

I had. Sometimes it's like looking into the future. Sometimes it's like seeing things I should know. So I certainly wasn't surprised. And it certainly paid off in the case of my husband, although we divorced about ten years later.

FRANCES, FROM THE MIDLANDS, describes a presentiment she had of a violent robbery at her home.

We were asleep in bed, my husband and I. Suddenly I woke up, sat up in the bed like a shot, terrified out of my wits, freezing cold, paralysed with fear and fright. It was a little after two o'clock in the early morning. There wasn't a sound, everything was quiet.

I pushed my husband and I said, 'Waken up! There is something wrong!' He said, 'What?' I said, 'There's something awful happening! I don't know what it is but it is awful!' The hair literally stood up on the back of my head. He said, 'You're having a nightmare.'

He jumped up, opened the blinds, looked out and couldn't see anything. I was still sitting in the bed, hugging myself, absolutely shaking and horrified. He ran into all the other rooms and looked out. He couldn't hear anything or see anything. He said, 'There's nobody there. It must have been just a nightmare.'

He got back into bed and went to sleep again. But I sat up for ages afterwards, horror-stricken, paralysed and unable to move. My bedroom, which was my haven, felt alien. There was nothing familiar or comforting about it. All my security systems had blown.

I felt there was something awful happening. I couldn't have got out of the bed if you asked me. It was like as if I was waiting for something but what it was I hadn't a clue. I can't explain the sense of evil.

Fifteen minutes later, at exactly half-past-two, I heard a little 'woof' from the dog in the kitchen and the next thing all hell broke loose. There was a crash and everything went haywire. An axe came through the plate glass window in the hall and another at the back door. Robbers burst in.

They shot my husband. He put his hands up against our bedroom door and they shot through the door. Two bullets went through his liver. He lost his spleen and part of his pancreas, the bottom of his lung and stomach.

I was hurt as well, pushed around badly and I injured my neck and my knee and had to have a lot of surgery, with a knee-joint replaced and so on. They stole our money. They shot our dog. But, strangely, that wasn't as frightening as the half-hour or so before.

I will never forget it. I will never forget the experience of waiting. I sensed the evil. I could feel it. It was so potent that it nearly smelled. I knew that something evil was coming. Something bad was going to happen. And the thought that went through my mind was, 'Nothing will ever be the same again!'

KATHLEEN LAWLESS, FROM COUNTY WICKLOW, relates how she, her daughters and her son had strange premonitions leading up to the death of her husband, John, on New Year's Day 2009.

My husband, John, was 66 years old and still working. He had gone for heart tests the previous August. His local doctor had detected a murmur so they did all the tests. They all came back clear. They said everything was normal. He was so fit. He didn't smoke and he drank very little. He ate well and he went for check-ups every six months. He really looked after himself.

He worked throughout the Christmas in the garden. He walked a lot, as well, including one four-mile or five-mile walk just a few days before he died. We had no indication that anything was wrong or that anything was going to happen. We had no idea that John was unwell or anything.

On New Year's Eve we were both at home. The weather was nice. John worked in the garden all day. I had been out shopping. I came in and was doing the usual chores around the house. Everything was normal. We were planning to go out to the golf club that night.

Around four o'clock this sudden black depression hit me. I felt completely down. I was as down as I could possibly be. It was a dreadful black feeling. It was like being in a room that was painted black. It was really, really bad. I didn't know what to do. I kept saying to myself, 'What is wrong with me?'

I was going around in circles. I knew I had to be ready to go out at a certain time but my mind was black. I never get depressed and I had no reason to feel that way. I had never been like this before. I didn't say it to anyone, not even to John. I kept it to myself. The depression lasted until about seven o'clock, for about three hours, and then it lifted.

My two daughters experienced things that were very, very strange as well. My second-eldest daughter Clodagh, who was 35 and married, got this dreadful feeling at her home. She and my husband were very close and she would nearly be talking to him on the phone every day. But she hadn't seen him most of that week, since St. Stephen's Day, because we had been away in Newry one day and down in Wicklow another day. She had only spoken to him on the phone.

That afternoon, on New Year's Eve, she got very agitated and uptight. She was in bad humour and didn't know why. She felt she had to get out of the house and call up to see us. A voice inside her head kept urging her to call up, even though she had been on the phone to me and to her dad that afternoon. Her husband told her, 'Just go.' So she went out and got into the car around half-four.

She remembers getting into the car and talking to herself out loud, saying, 'What is wrong with me? Why am I like this? Why am I being told to call up to Mam and Dad?' She only lived a few minutes away. She first went to the shops with her daughter and when she was back in the car the same thing was in her head, 'Call up! Call up!'

She looked at the clock in the car and she knew we were due to go out to the golf club. So she said, 'I can't call up now because I'll delay them with the baby. It's not really fair.' She felt that the baby would distract us. So she came to a round-about not far from our house, turned the car around and went back.

She wasn't happy turning back because she still had this feeling. It's something she had never had before. She didn't know what was wrong with her. It really scared her. It was incredible and it had never happened to her before or it never happened since.

My youngest daughter, Fiona, who was 26 and lived at home, also had a strange feeling. On New Year's Eve she said to the girls who worked with her in her office, 'I have a feeling that 2009 is going to be a bad year for me.' The girls said, 'Don't be silly.' She said, 'I just have that feeling.'

My son, Colin, also said later that he had some very bad nightmares over that Christmas week. He said he saw himself going out to buy a suit for a funeral and he saw himself up at the top row of the church. It was all very strange.

On New Year's Eve night we left as planned for the golf club and John never looked as well. He looked great. There was no indication that anything was wrong. We met up with a couple who are very close to us. We had a meal. John was grand and in great form that night. The only indication I had was that, when we came home at around two o'clock, he said, 'I'm going on up to bed. I'm a bit tired.'

I woke up the next morning and I thought John was having a nightmare. He was breathing strangely and seemed distressed. We were planning to go down to Wexford for the day and the following day we were planning to go down to friends in Kilkenny. But, in fact, John was having a massive heart attack. That was at about quarter-past-eight and he died on that New Year's Day.

It was really extraordinary that the three of us had those experiences the day before. There was no explanation for my depression. I never, ever had anything like it before. Fiona's experience was strange too. She had such a bad feeling about the year ahead and she lost her father the following day.

She also lost her job although she got another one. And she had a horse that died. She was broken-hearted after that too – she had lost another soul mate. It was extraordinary. The girls she worked with said they were shocked by what she had said. They remarked on that at the funeral.

My other daughter, Clodagh, still can't explain how she felt. She now worries that if something like it ever happens again, she will panic. She is terrified that it will happen again and that she will feel that something bad is going to happen to someone close to her. She worries she will feel they are going to die.

There's another thing – when we were in Newry, the day before New Year's Eve, we were in Debenhams and John said, 'I think I'll buy a new coat.' I said, 'You have two good coats. Why don't you buy a suit?' So he said, 'OK.' He bought a suit. And the rest is history – he was buried in it.

Looking back, it's all so extraordinary. I can't explain it. There's no explanation. It's all so strange and puzzling. We still talk about it but we are all still baffled and we still don't know what the reasons are. These things never happened to us before. But they happened on New Year's Eve 2008 and I definitely know we felt John's death coming.

SHEELAGH, FROM COUNTY ANTRIM, had a preview of a car crash which happened in 1956.

My husband and I weren't very long married at the time. We had got married in August of 1956. We were in our very early 20s and were living in our own home between Lisburn and Belfast. We had a pale blue Ford Anglia. We didn't go out much because we were newly married and didn't have the money. But we sometimes went to the cinema.

One night, around September, I had this dream. I was a dreamer all my life. This one was very vivid and real. We were in the car and we were driving to the cinema. It was dark. My husband was doing the driving. We were going to the Regal, which was about four or five miles away. There wasn't much traffic in those days. There weren't many cars on the road.

We stopped at the lights at Balmoral. All of a sudden there was this bit of a bang. A car behind us had not stopped on time and he hit us. My husband got out. There was no damage so he got back in again. We drove off when the lights turned green. Eventually, as we approached the cinema, we slowed down. We needed to turn right to park the car, so my husband indicated right.

This time there was this almighty bang. My husband got out and there was some damage done to the car. The other driver got out as well. He was very aggressive. He pushed my husband and knocked him down. He sort of punched him. I had, at this stage, also got out of the car and was observing all this. My husband was on the ground.

There were other people who were observing what was happening as well. One of them must have rung the police because they arrived quickly. They got the story from both of us and from somebody else who had observed it. The police said, 'We will take care of it.' My husband got back into the car. I got in. We parked the car and we went off to the pictures. And that was the end of the dream.

I remembered the dream the next morning and told my husband. He looked at me and said, 'Oh! You were dreaming again.' That was more or less it. I never really thought anything about it again. But it was very realistic. I could see the cinema, the houses, the road, the car, everything. It was just as if I was there and it was really happening.

About six or eight weeks later, around November, we decided to go to the cinema. I think it was a Friday night. It was dark, around seven o'clock. We went to the Regal but I can't remember what film was on. We left our house and arrived at the lights. They were red so we stopped. This driver was behind us and he gave our car a bit of a bump. My husband got out and looked. There was no damage so he got back in again. The lights changed and we moved off.

It was less than five minutes from the lights to the Regal cinema. We were slowing down as we approached it. My husband was indicating to turn right. The next thing this man came along – it was the same driver – and he hit our car a right good thump. My husband got out and went to the back of the car. There was a bit of damage done, a bit of a dent at the rear.

The other driver had got out of the car by this time. He had black hair and he wasn't very tall. He seemed to be very aggressive. I got out as well. I remember I was thinking, 'This can't be happening. This is ridiculous. My dream is coming true.' I was a wee bit frightened as well. I thought, 'My God! Don't tell me I am psychic or whatever.'

Just as I got out I saw the man punching my husband and knocking him down onto the road. As a result, my husband got a little bruise just below his left eye. The police then came along very quickly. We don't know whether someone rang for them or whether there was a patrol car in the area. But there certainly were people about and maybe someone in a nearby house had seen what happened. Maybe they rang for the police from their house phone – don't forget that nobody had mobile phones in those days.

The police stopped and got out. They had a word with my husband. They also had a word with the other driver, who definitely must have had some sort of drink on him. The police then said, 'We'll take care of this. We'll attend to this.' We said, 'Right. OK.' So we parked the car and went off to the cinema, just as we did in the dream. And we never heard anything about it again. The police never contacted us.

My husband was absolutely amazed. He said to me, 'My God! Your dream!' I said, 'Yes! There you are!' He was shocked and absolutely astounded. He said, 'If you dream anything like that again, don't ever tell me anything about it.' Any time I would dream something later on and I'd go to tell him, he would say, 'I don't want to know.'

I used to think about the dream over the years. I would think, 'Wasn't it a weird thing for me to have the dream and for it to happen?' I wondered why I had dreamt it. Had I seen into the future? I wondered was it caused by being psychic or from something else in your mind. I really don't know. I couldn't honestly say why it happened. But somehow I saw the future.

I never had a dream about a car crash again. It only happened once. But I can still remember it today, it was so vivid. I can still see it all now as I talk to you. Everything has changed – the cinema is gone and the road has changed too. There's a flyover now but the traffic-lights are still there. Our little Anglia is gone too. But the memory stays on. I will never forget it. I can hardly really believe it myself but I know it happened. It was absolutely astounding.

Bríd, from County Clare, developed an unusual ability to foresee events. It lasted for more than two decades.

I started getting premonitions when I was aged 19. I would have a few serious ones every year. They nearly always came true. But I was also having lots of little premonitions about something. They would come in a flash and they would go in a flash. They would be very brief. They would leave me very quickly but they would seem to come back and they might linger.

There was one occasion, back in the early 1980s, where I spotted this child belonging to a very large family. I don't know why I picked him out. I didn't know him very well. I remember saying, 'Just supposing he had an accident and something happened.' I thought, 'You don't know what is around the corner.' That was the end of that.

Years later I saw him again when he was in his late teens. I remember it was a beautiful day. I was sitting down and saw him walking by. He passed where I was sitting. He caught my eye again. I got this very strong urge. I said, 'He is a very special child. I must tell his mother to mind him. I must ring her and tell her.' Unfortunately I never told her and never acted on it. We eventually got news that he was killed in a tragic accident.

I remember a different occasion, when I got this awful feeling. It was a Monday morning, about 11 o'clock. I was at the sink, washing and peeling potatoes. My husband came in and said, 'I would murder a cup of tea.' I suddenly turned around and said, 'I don't know what's wrong but I cannot move this doom and gloom.' He said, 'Don't be talking about doom and gloom.'

I had never experienced anything like it before. I wanted to cry but I couldn't. I was wondering, 'What's going to happen? Something is definitely going to happen.' I had this quivery feeling in my arms. I said to my husband, 'Why do I think our lives are going to change today and they will never be the same again?'

At about one o'clock a phone call came to tell us that my mother-in-law had got a blackout. It turned out that she actually had got a brain haemorrhage. She was in the hospital. My husband went up to her and he rang me to say she had died. When he came home he asked me, 'What did you say to me today?' I told him again. And he said, 'Well, that's what that was about!'

There was another time, when I predicted my father-in-law's death. He called by to our house. It was a Thursday afternoon. We were having tea in the kitchen. There were other people in the house at the time. Eventually the other people left and I was alone with my father-in-law. His wife was already dead and he was telling me how lonely he was.

Then he decided to leave. We walked out into our hallway. He turned back to me and gave me a hug before he left. I suddenly said to myself, 'Why do I think that I will never see this man again?' Two days later, around two o'clock on the Saturday afternoon, we got a phone call. It was a neighbour of my father-in-law's and he said my father-in-law was after having a very bad accident. He had been killed.

There was yet another occasion, where a girl I worked with called to me. She said, 'I have some photographs to show you.' She showed them to me. There were four or five people in one shot. I would have known them well and was friendly with them even though they were older than me. 'Look at them,' she said. 'Don't they look great?' I said, 'Yes, they do.'

Then she pointed to one person on the left. 'Doesn't she look marvellous?' she said. All I wanted to say was, 'Please take that photograph away! She looks terrible!' This girl in the photograph was in the full of her health. But I knew immediately, 'This looks like someone that is going to die!' I knew something was going to happen. A little over a week later she was involved in a dreadful car crash and she died.

There have been loads of other things that have happened over the years. The serious ones lasted into my early 40s. I can always remember what I was wearing when I would have them. Everything is so clear. Even now, as I am thinking about them, I can really remember everything that took place at the time. But I haven't had any serious premonitions for a long time. The last serious one I had was back in 1990.

When I look back, I often ask myself, 'Why didn't I do something? Why didn't I act? What prevented me from acting?' But I never acted on them. That haunts me a bit. I feel shame and embarrassment when I think of that. There have been times over the years where my life would have been changed if I opened my mouth because of things I had predicted. But I never did anything. I think it still wouldn't have stopped what happened. I suppose you can't change destiny.

I often wonder if it is a gift or a curse or whatever. And I wonder how I developed the ability in the first place. When I was a child I was often brought to wakes. I also heard lots of stories about ghosts and hauntings. I sometimes wonder if those things tapped into some potential that was there and it lingered on. But I also wonder if other people feel like this. And I suppose I have some power although I would never talk about it to anyone. I just tell myself that it is coming from a good force.

BERNADETTE, FROM COUNTY CORK, describes her mother's strange forewarning of another person's death in 1951.

There was a small hotel down the road from where my mother used to live. It was one of the main hotels in the town at the time. My mother was brought up in a house just above it. They would have looked down at the hotel. It was only a few minutes walk away, down a lane.

My family was very close to the family that owned the hotel. They were all brought up in the same area, with just the lane between them. They would have been together at school. They emigrated together. They all knew each other well.

The hotel was run by a mighty woman who was a great worker, fluent in Irish and had a big family. The hotel was a great place, full of activity and people. One member of her family was in New Zealand. Another one, a son, was in New York. His name was Seán. He was aged 21 and wasn't long in America. He had only emigrated a few months before.

My mother was about 20 at the time and was living at home. She was working out the road in one of the factories. She knew all the family who owned the hotel, including the son who was in America although he would have been a bit older than her.

One day she was on her way home from work, during daytime. It was 11 March 1951. The hotel had a side entrance and you'd go straight into the kitchen. The son, Seán, instead of being in New York, was at the door. He was standing at the doorway, dressed in a tweed suit and with his hand in his pocket. He said, 'Hello, Mary. How are you?' She said, 'God! Hello.' She was amazed to see him back from America.

She went off home and said, 'Seán, from the hotel, is home from America.' They said, 'What? The family never mentioned that he was coming home. That's great.' They were surprised because, at that time, if you were coming home there would be a big discussion about the dates and everything. Trips home were very unusual. It was a totally different era. They were particularly surprised that the family had never said he was coming. They thought it was strange.

The following day they got the news that Seán had been shot dead in New York. The news was delivered by telegram. Everybody was shocked. But no one was more shocked than my mother. It was only the previous day – the day that he was shot – that she had said she saw him by the hotel.

We all grew up with that story at home, all the time. We often spoke about it. My father would say, 'Mary, tell us that story again.' When my mother's sisters would come home from America they'd talk about the old days and they'd say, 'Mary, do you remember what happened with Seán?'

I talked to my aunt about it recently. She remembered it well. She was at home the day my mother arrived in to say she had met Seán down by the hotel. She remembers that she got her confirmation at the same time as he did. When I spoke to her she said, 'We'll never forget it. There have only been two or three strange things that I have seen happen in life and that's one of them.'

The woman who owned the hotel lived well into her 90s but she eventually died. The name of her son who died in America, Seán, is engraved on the family headstone, saying that he is buried in New York. They never brought him home for burial. The headstone simply points out that he died on 11 March 1951.

As for my mother, she is dead now about five years and she never had any doubt about what happened, that he said hello to her. Why would she have said it out of the blue? She was in her 20s at the time, young and healthy, and it was daylight. She said he was crystal clear. The only explanation she had was that it was his soul passing over and he came to say goodbye.

COLETTE, FROM BELFAST, was advised of the imminent death of her mother who passed away in early 1990.

I was in bed one Sunday night. It was just an ordinary Sunday night back in November 1989. I didn't have drink taken or anything like that. I was asleep. My husband was on the other side of me. He was asleep too. I suddenly felt a tap on my right shoulder. I opened my eyes and there was this woman standing there. She wasn't floating or anything – she was just standing there.

The woman had black curly hair and a lovely face. She was young. She was about 30 years of age and very beautiful. I couldn't make out who she was. I didn't recognise her. She said, 'Your mother is going to die in ten days!' We had a light on in the landing, because the kids were small then, and it shone into the room. I could see her clearly.

We also had a light above our bed and I just pulled it on. I shouted at my husband and woke him up. When I looked back to where she had been, she was gone. My husband said, 'You've been dreaming.' I said, 'No. I haven't. There's a woman in the room.'

The next morning I told my sister what had happened. She said, 'For goodness sake! There's nothing wrong with Mammy.' My sister lived with her. However, from that day on I started watching Mammy. I started to say, 'She's not well.'

Eventually, on New Year's Day, my mother started to complain about her back. My husband and I would always take her out for a meal. She normally loved to do that. But she said, 'No. I don't think so. I don't really want to go out.' I immediately said, 'This is it. She's not well. She's going to die.' I knew it.

She was taken into hospital. It was in February, a couple of months after the woman had come to me in my room. The doctor said, 'We are not looking for anything sinister. It's just a hernia. Everything should be alright.' They operated on her. Afterwards everybody went off home from the hospital but I knew not to go home myself. A nurse came out and said, 'I thought you went home.' I said, 'No. I'm just waiting to see.'

The next thing my other sister came back to the hospital. She was the colour of death and she said, 'I've got an awful feeling that something is wrong.' She was the calm one. I would have been the hysterical one. Suddenly the doctor came up the stairs. He came up to me and said, 'I'm very, very sorry. Your mother had a hernia alright but she had cancer with it.'

My sister started cracking up. The nurse had to take her in and give her a cup of tea. But, somehow, I could take it because of what I had known. I asked the doctor, 'How long does she have?' He said, 'About two weeks.' I said, 'I don't want her to know. I want her out of here because her wish always was to die at home with her family around her.' He said, 'I will have to tell her what she has.' But I said, 'Please, don't.'

I didn't go back in to see my mother that day because I knew that she would see on my face that I knew. The next morning, however, I went back down to the hospital at eight o'clock. Mammy said to me, 'Do you know that stuff they use to knock you out with?' I said, 'Yes.' She said, 'I had the biggest nightmare after they gave it to me. I saw everybody there and they were crying.'

Eventually we took Mammy home. I was extremely upset by what was going on. My mother and I were very close. We took her on holidays. She went with us everywhere. Everybody used to worry and say to me, 'What's going to happen when your mother dies?' But she did die. She died on St. Valentine's Day. And from the day she entered the hospital to the day she died was exactly ten days.

During the wake a cousin of mine came in and she pulled out the memory card of my mammy's sister, who had died almost 20 years earlier. I only remember my aunt from when she was older. But there she was in the photo when she was about 30. And that was the same woman who came to me in the bedroom and told me that my mother would die in ten days.

It was all so strange. My aunt was a really lovely lady. She always had a couple of bob and was so posh. She was the only posh one in our family who would say 'your mother.' It was always 'your mother.' She would say, 'I'm going to tell your mother you are running amok.' The rest of us would say 'my mammy' or 'my ma.' And that's what she said when she came to me – 'your mother.' When I put two and two together, I knew, 'That's who told me. It was my auntie.'

I just knew something was going to happen. I honestly knew it was coming because it had been told to me. After Mammy started complaining I knew there was definitely something wrong. It nearly killed me because I was so close to her, but it prepared me. At least I had a forewarning and it helped me immensely.

EILEEN MEENAN, FROM COUNTY LOUTH, details the strange events that occurred around her husband Sam's death. He was aged 52.

My husband had the most perfect Christmas back in 2007. We had just moved into a new house. He went and got a new microwave, even though we didn't need one. He got a new freezer. He changed the kettle. He did the Christmas shopping. He did all this while waiting on a hip-replacement and in terrible pain.

Two days after Christmas he said he was tired. He wasn't really eating very well. He went over to the shop for a salad roll and I said, 'At least he's eating that.' When he came home he called me. I said, 'Yeah?' He said, 'Take that! Quick! I think I'm going to be sick!' He said, 'I don't feel well at all!' He thought he was going to pass out and he was shivering.

He went up to bed and I told him to lie down in the back room where the two wee boys, Kevin and Leo, slept. He lay down in one of the beds there. He came up and down the stairs a good few times throughout the day. He said, 'I can't shake off this tiredness or coldness.' I thought he was getting a cold or something.

The last time he came down I was sitting in the kitchen and listening to some Irish singers, including Sonny Knowles. I was sitting and thinking and wishing he was well. I said, 'Do you want a cup of tea?' He said, 'No, if you don't mind. I'm dead tired. I think I'll just go on up.' This had never happened before.

My heart plunged. I went to the door and I looked down the hall after him. I said, 'Are you sure you are OK?' He turned and said, 'My leg is killing me!' He looked in pain and he went off to bed saying, 'I'll stay in the wee bedroom with one of the boys and you take the other boy.'

In that moment an awful sadness came over me. I couldn't shake it off. I sat in the kitchen and the music was on but my heart wasn't in it. This sadness was coming over me. I had rung my mum earlier and I felt I couldn't ring her again. I just stayed listening to the music.

Time was flying by. I looked at the clock and it said half-one. Then, at ten-to-two, I looked up at the left corner of the room where this wee shelf was. Sitting on it was this photo of my dad who had passed away. My husband had also put a photo up there of his mother who had passed away. My husband had placed a Christmas card next to his mum's photo and I had a card with a robin on the front next to my dad's.

As I looked at the card to my dad, there was no photo of a robin on it anymore. Instead I could see a vision of a girl with dark hair. The face was covering the robin. And the face was me! It looked exactly like me. I was as sober as a judge. I didn't drink. I am a teetotaller. And I started to get scared.

I started moving the curtains to see if something was shining on the area. I sat down and when I looked up again it was still there. I saw the time on the clock and I noticed that it stayed there until a couple of minutes to two. It then left and was gone, like it had never been there before.

I sat there thinking. I felt I had to pray for something so I prayed. I never knew what it was that I was praying for. I felt I had to be calm for some reason. I thought it all had something to do with my dad. I felt my dad was with me. Time flew by and the next thing I looked at the clock and it was quarter-past-three. I said, 'I'd better get up. I'd better go to bed.'

I went down the hall and went to go up the stairs. When I got my foot on the third step, suddenly this smell hit me. I wondered, 'What is this?' I started getting afraid. The only time I ever remember getting that smell was going to a wake, when I was young, after a man died. It was the exact same smell and it terrified me.

I went on up the stairs and I looked in the room where he was. There was a wee rainbow light going around the room, with a wee nightlight, and it changed blue, green, red, all different colours. I saw him in the bed. I thought he might be awake because he had been up and down to bed a lot so I said, 'Goodnight!' But he said nothing. I thought, 'He is fast asleep.'

I went into my own bed and left the door open. I was annoyed by the smell I got on the stairs. Suddenly all the peaceful feeling I had down in the kitchen was gone. I was sitting in the bed and couldn't sleep. I was afraid. I was getting this awful feeling. I felt something was going to happen and I kept asking, 'What is it?'

Around five-to-four I was sort of dozing and the next thing I heard footsteps. They seemed to come straight in from the window in the hall. I could hear a quick step going right over the wooden floor. It was like a woman's shoe or something. It went over the floor and into that back bedroom.

I jumped. I was absolutely terrified. I hopped up out of bed. I wondered, 'Is there somebody going to the toilet?' But nobody passed my door to get to the toilet and they would have to pass the door. The steps just stopped, gone. I was so afraid that I didn't go out to look. Strangely, a sort of calmness came over me again. I felt I didn't have to be afraid anymore.

Eventually, somewhere after six o'clock, I heard the wee boy calling, 'Daddy! Daddy! Bo Bo!' He got no answer, which was not like his dad. He was always on the button. I heard him saying it again, 'Daddy! Daddy! Bo Bo!' Nothing! I jumped out of bed, terrified. I thought, 'He's not well at all.'

I went into the room and saw the baby, Leo, up on top of

his daddy. He was on his chest and he had put his wee baby blanket from the pram, which he had obviously brought to bed as a comfort, up over his daddy. He said, 'I've already given Daddy a blanket and he's still very cold.'

Then my other wee boy, Kevin, came running in behind me. He kept saying, 'Stop staring at me, Daddy!' He started screaming. I hit the floor and must have passed out at the bottom of the bed. I got up and I was just staring. I couldn't go over to him, with fear. One of the boys was holding his hand and the other was on his chest. I said to one, 'Give your daddy a kiss. Say goodnight.' And he did. I told the other, 'Close his eyes.' I was thinking of meningitis or that he was going into some sort of coma.

I just flew out the front door, with the children following me. I never thought of mobile phones or the house phone, nothing. There was a taxi rank across the road but there wasn't a light on – it mustn't have been time for opening yet. I ran down the middle of the street and I didn't know what to do. I didn't know where I was going.

This nurse came out of her house across the road and she said, 'Where are you going at this hour? What's wrong?' I said, 'I can't get Sam awake! He won't wake up!' I didn't know what I was saying. She said, 'Steady up! Steady up! Come on! Come on! Keep calm!'

She came into the house and said, 'All the children into the kitchen! Do not come upstairs!' It seemed to take forever. I thought she was going to reassure me and say, 'It's meningitis.' Instead she came down and said, 'I'm sorry. There's no easy way to tell you. He's gone!' And my world was just shattered.

The children suddenly started screaming. The older one was screaming, 'Daddy! Daddy!' The younger one didn't know what he was crying for. I can still hear the haunting sound. I just looked over at the Christmas tree. And I looked up at the shelf and I thought, 'So that's what it was all about!'

It turned out that my husband had a clot in his leg. That might explain the cold feeling he had. I only heard recently, from somebody who was talking about blood clots, that one of the symptoms is being cold. I was thinking, 'He was always in a sun top.' If I had known about the symptom I would have had him up at the doctor. But you can't blame yourself.

Afterwards I thought, 'That was my dad helping me that night.' That was my head and shoulders on the card, up next to his shoulder. I think he was being a 'shoulder' for me. I feel he was saying, 'I'm there for you.' That's all I can make of it. I think he was helping me and he knew something was coming. Whether people believe me or not, I don't care. As God may strike me dead, it definitely did happen. No one can ever tell me that it didn't.

MARY, FROM COUNTY CORK, believes that her deceased father came with a warning shortly before the death of her sister.

My sister, Therese, was a very good person. Although she was very abrupt, forthright and straight, she was also very honest and kind. She didn't drink or smoke and she exercised all the time. She went to bed early and got up early and walked to work in the morning. She loved sitting and looking out at the sea. She was very contented.

Most girls are very attached to their mother but Therese adored my father. She was very upset when he died. She also had no interest in money. 'I don't want anything,' she used to say. She had very few possessions even though she and her husband were very comfortably off and weren't short of anything. On one occasion she called her son and daughter down from Dublin and said, 'Take what you want. I only need this and this and this.' It was almost as if she had a premonition of something to come.

One day – it was in February or March 2001 – I came home at lunchtime. I was sitting in my kitchen. I was about to have a sandwich and a cup of tea. I was reading my book and I thought, 'This is great. I'm really looking forward to this.' I was getting stuck into my book when all of a sudden my father came into my head. I started thinking about him and his birthday coming up in April.

The next thing this feeling came over me. I have never experienced anything like it. It was beautiful and warm. It was a wonderful feeling but multiplied by a million. It started on the top of my head and came down my shoulders. It was like when you are cold and someone comes and wraps a warm blanket around you. There was a definite purity in what I felt.

I knew Daddy was with me. I said, 'Daddy! You are here, aren't you? I know you are here!' I looked up the kitchen fully expecting to see him. But he wasn't there at all. I was very disappointed. Then everything left me. The whole feeling was gone in the blink of an eye. Everything disappeared. It may have lasted for less than a minute.

I nearly cried. I didn't want it to go. I said, 'Come back! Come back!' The feeling was really intense. It was wonderful. I then started doubting myself. I was wondering, 'Did that happen?' I wondered was I just being over-imaginative. But I wasn't. I did feel it. I really felt it. It was a feeling that went right to my core.

Not long afterwards, in May, Therese got sick. She had come in to me one day and said, 'I've just been to the doctor. I must go for tests. I'm very short of breath going up steps.' It turned out to be a problem with her heart. She had three major blockages behind the heart. It is one of the most dangerous places to have blockages. She went into hospital and we went in to see her. When she came home she was terribly weak.

One day some of our family went to visit her at her house. My sister was there and my niece was there with her children. It was a beautiful summer's day. We went swimming and we had a cup of tea. Eventually all the others left. I stayed with her. I felt she didn't want me to leave. She wanted me to stay. I was sitting directly across from her and I was looking into her face.

I wondered, 'Will I bring up that Daddy was around?' I had slightly said it to her before but she didn't say anything. So I told her what had happened. I was expecting her to say, 'Oh! For goodness sake! Don't be silly!' Instead she said, 'That was for me!' I thought she would have told me, 'You are being ridiculous!' But far from it – instead she insisted, 'That was for me!'

A week later, in June, she died. She was aged 58. She was at home and she was getting weaker and weaker. She was constantly having heart failure. One day she went off for a shower. Her husband was about to go and get the papers but he hung around. He heard a thud. She had fallen in the shower. The doctor found a small pulse and he worked on her all the way to Cork in an ambulance. When she got to Cork they put her on life support but it was no good. She was gone. It was all over.

I really believe my father came to me. I thought at the time I might have been imagining it but I now know I wasn't. I felt him. I think he came to let us know that something was coming. I had thought at the time it was something to do with Therese's sickness, that he was saying that everything would be alright, but I never thought it was about her death.

Looking back, I think Daddy was coming for her. I think Daddy was preparing us for something. He was always a rock. He may have come to me because I was the youngest. I really just don't know. But he was definitely coming about Therese, telling us that there was something bad about to happen. I am sure of that.

PATRICIA PLUNKETT, FROM COUNTY MAYO, foretold her nephew's death long before he was even born.

My sister used to live down in County Wicklow, in a beautiful house. I used to go up regularly to visit her. It was a lovely location. She had a big sitting-room, looking out onto the main road. One day I was in that sitting-room and I was looking out the window. There was this awful coldness in the room even though it was summertime. It was always a cold room.

Suddenly I had this clear vision. In the vision there were people standing from the front door down to the gate. They were standing on both sides of the path. I saw this little white coffin being carried out and brought down to a car. I said, 'God! This is ridiculous. This is awful.' I shook myself and said, 'Don't be ridiculous.' I walked out of the sitting-room.

I thought of my sister's little girl. She had one child at the time. I thought, 'They are living on a main road!' I said to my sister, 'You ought to put a lock on the gate! Don't ever let her out!' I was scared about what could happen to the little girl although I never said anything to my sister about what I had seen. I kept it to myself.

A couple of years later my sister had a little boy. He was a healthy child and everything was grand. That was the case until he was two years old. He started getting sick. On one occasion he was staying with me and he was vomiting. She took him home. Eventually, after three weeks, they discovered he had a brain tumour. He had the tumour removed and they said it was cancerous.

They said he could live a year or four years or ten years – they really didn't know. As it happened, he just lived until the following November. He was really sick on a Wednesday but I couldn't get off work. I said to my sister, 'Whisper in his ear. Tell him to wait for me. I'll be down on Saturday.' She kept telling him to wait. We arrived at three o'clock and he died at six. He died in my arms.

The strange thing was that it was in that same room that he was laid out. When he was being brought to the church on the Tuesday morning, I was actually one of the people in the line down to the gate. And the white coffin was brought down from the house. It was only then that I remembered that this was exactly how it was in my vision. They have sold the house since. But, up to the time they did, the house was never cold again.

EILEEN, FROM COUNTY LOUTH, had a strange premonition of her grandmother's death back in 1988.

My parents came originally from both County Donegal and County Tyrone but they moved in the mid-1950s to Glasgow. It was a time of recession. They got married there and they had all of us there. My granny and many other relatives were still living in Donegal. Our family eventually moved back to Ireland and we settled in Dundalk. It was there, one Saturday night, that I had the strangest premonition.

I was living in a flat at the time and on the Saturday night I had a 'dream'. I remember it was the last day of April. My bed is tight into the wall but I woke up around four or five in the morning and there was a fellow standing over my bed, with curly hair. He came to my bed but he didn't talk. He just called me with his hands. He kept on waving his hands and I followed him.

He took me to a headstone. It was light and it was sunny. It was beautiful and warm. It was most peaceful. He rested his hands on the headstone. He smiled although he never spoke. He stayed with me, to reassure me. Then he vanished. I was left saying, 'Where did he go to? He was so nice.'

I went home on the Sunday and I told it to my mum. I said, 'I had this awful, weird dream last night.' When I told my mum about it she said, 'What? You are raving. You must be hallucinating.' I said, 'I'm not. I'll draw his face, if I have to.' I told her what he looked like.

That night my dad left me back home. I had this feeling that I should not get ready to go to work the next day. I felt I should get ready to go somewhere else because some sad thing was going to happen. I got a black shirt out and I stood there ironing. I didn't know what I was getting ready for. But I knew I was getting ready for something.

The next thing I heard the sound of my dad's car coming around the corner. I knew the sound of the engine. I heard it coming towards the door. It was just after ten-past-twelve, just past midnight. I ran and opened the door and I knew, 'This is bad!'

My dad said, 'We've just got word that Granny is after taking a massive heart attack and she has died.' I later said to my mother, 'Remember, I told you I had this dream.' She said, 'Tell me about it again.'

We went to Donegal and we were down in my granny's house. There were lots of people there. They were all in this big sitting-room in the back. In the sitting-room I happened to look and there was this photograph there. It was of the boy with the curly hair!

182

I said, 'Where's my mother?' She was elsewhere talking to somebody else in one of the other rooms. I eventually found her and told her, 'That was the person I saw.' She said that he was a son who was lost years ago. That was him. I also later said it to my aunt and I told her, 'I sensed something was coming.' I didn't know what it was but I definitely had a sign.

What happened was incredible but it doesn't frighten me. I felt a bit frightened that Saturday night when the image first came to me. But otherwise I don't feel any fear. I feel you shouldn't be afraid of the dead. I think, 'What is going to harm you? They are all peaceful.' I honestly think, 'We shouldn't be afraid.'

MARIE, FROM COUNTY WATERFORD, had an instinctive premonition that her father, who was most unwell, was about to die.

My father was dying at home. He was living second-next-door to where we live and we cared for him. He wasn't well for about two weeks but his heart was so sound he lived on. One particular night I had put on some chickens to cook in my house. I went up to check them. I opened the oven. Suddenly something said into my ear, 'Go! Go!'

I just ran out the door and ran down the road to his house. I left the oven open, with the chickens hanging out. I left the front door open too. I ran into the house. My brother had been with him and he was there. I said, 'He's going! He's going!' He said, 'How do you mean?' I said, 'I know he's going!' With that he drew his last breath.

I just can't explain it. Something had whispered into my ear, 'Go! Just leave!' We had been waiting for it to happen for a while. And I desperately wanted to be there. It was extraordinary. I just had time to sit down and hold his hand and he was gone.

ROSE MARY, FROM DUBLIN, believes that animals also have unusual predictive and sensory powers. One of her stories concerns a family dog, the other a cat.

My mother had a cat and the two of them were the best of friends. They were very close and were side by side all the time. My mother and the cat had a routine. She served the cat's meals three times a day. She got supper at nine o'clock. The minute nine o'clock came, the cat stood up and more or less said, 'Time for supper!' It was useful because it reminded my mother to take her pill at nine o'clock.

Every afternoon my mother went for a lie-down. She had one of those old-fashioned satin quilts on the bed. A special cardigan was always put down on the bed for the cat. It was the same routine every afternoon, at around three o'clock or whatever. The two of them would then have their snooze.

Eventually my mother got a heart attack. She was aged 89. Luckily it happened when I was home for lunch. I got the doctor and he said, 'Get an ambulance!' But my mother said, 'I want to die in my own bed. I'm not going to hospital.' So I said, 'We can get nurses in to look after her.' And that's what we did.

She was five days ill in bed. Everybody came to see her, even a couple of people who maybe she hadn't been that close to. It was a great consolation. Strangely for those five days the cat would not go near her. The cat would not come up to the bedroom but would lie downstairs. That was the only thing that was troubling my mother. She kept asking, 'Where is the cat?' She couldn't go down and see the cat because she was told not to go downstairs.

Eventually my mother fell into a coma. I was elsewhere in the house but I could hear this deep breathing. I went in to her and found that her book had fallen out of her hands although her glasses were still on her nose. I phoned my next-door neighbour and told her my mother had gone into a coma. She came in to help. My mother's breathing became more widely spaced. A breath would come and then another breath would come. You would wonder, 'Is this the last breath?' But then another breath would come again.

Suddenly, very close to the end, the cat came running up the stairs and into the room as if she had been called urgently. You felt she was pounding up the stairs. The cat jumped up on this wooden chair beside the bed. She drew herself up like one of those Egyptian cats with the long necks. She looked up to a place about three or four feet above where my mother's body was lying. She kept at that for about 30 seconds and then ran downstairs.

It was strange where she looked. She wasn't looking up at the ceiling – it was a place about three feet above my mother. My neighbour and I both witnessed what had happened. My neighbour confirmed it. I think the cat was looking at where my mother's spirit was rising up out of her body. And I'm convinced that she saw my mother's spirit leaving. I think animals are sensitive to things like that.

There was another story in our family, which happened long before I was born. It took place in 1915, during the First World War. My father came from Derry, where his family had a business. His brother was out in Donegal one day in the middle of August. There was a crowd of them there and they all went in for a swim. Unfortunately he drowned. He was only 19. Making matters worse, they didn't find the body for a number of weeks.

My father had a little dog that he was very fond of. He had grown up with the dog. The minute his brother disappeared, the little dog started howling. He howled and he howled and he howled. My grandmother couldn't stand it. I suppose it was hard enough for them without the dog howling all the time. They actually had to put the dog down, which broke my father's heart. He not only lost his brother but also his dog.

My grandparents were convinced that the dog knew what had happened and that my uncle had drowned. Even though it had happened in Donegal and they lived in Derry, the dog sensed that he was dead. In fact, it turned out that the dog had started howling at the time my uncle had drowned, which was long before the news of the tragedy came through to Derry. It was something we talked about in our family all the time. So there certainly is something that animals can sense. I definitely believe that.

THERESA CORRIGAN, FROM COUNTY CAVAN, **heard knocking on her bedroom window shortly before her grandmother died. Her grandmother was 88 years old.**

My granny was in the hospital and she was elderly but she wasn't expected to die. She had taken a bit of a turn but it wasn't critical. She wasn't on her death-bed or anything. My mother was getting ready to take her home. I was pregnant with my first child at the time.

We live out in the country and we are fairly isolated. It's an old house. We had taken away a lot of the old sheds and the earth so there is very little around the house. It's very open. There are no trees or anything else nearby.

My husband farms and he got up to look at a cow that was calving. You know the way you'd have to be watching them in the springtime. But the cow was fine. My husband was getting back into bed and we were both awake. We were both sitting up. It was about three o'clock in the morning. I was setting the clock for another hour, to have another look at the cow.

Suddenly there were these loud knocks on the bedroom window. There are two windows and the knocks were on the front one, on the left. When we were in the bed, facing the door, it was the window to our left. It was like five or six sharp bangs. They were definitely on the glass. The noise was loud and it sounded like they were caused by a coin or something like that. We didn't get to analyse it as it happened.

At first we thought it was a neighbour across the road. We thought he might have seen the lights on and had a cow calving or whatever. My husband got up and walked around the house but he saw nobody. He came back in and said, 'There's nobody out there.' There definitely wasn't anyone around.

When my husband was gone out I thought of my grand-mother in hospital. I thought my husband would laugh if I told him when he came back in. But he didn't. We said a few prayers and I had a sort of sixth sense that it was something to do with her. I wasn't scared. I said, 'She didn't harm us when she was alive so why then would she harm us on her passing?'

I got up at seven o'clock the next morning and I rang the hospital. Granny hadn't been disturbed. She was still lying in the bed and she looked fine. The nurse just said, 'No. She's fine.' I rang my home place and my younger sisters were still there at the time. I told them what had happened and that I was worried. They said, 'Mam has gone up to feed her. We'll see what she says.'

My mother came back and she said, 'I think it's the end.' Granny must have got a turn or a stroke during the night. The nurses hadn't realised it when I rang. They only realised it later in the morning. They saw she wasn't well. Her face had gone to one side. She wasn't fit to eat. And she died at six o'clock that evening.

It was unreal. We just couldn't believe it. We said, 'My God! After all the things the older people have been saying and there we are after experiencing it ourselves!' I had heard stories like that when I was younger. Older people said they happened. It was very common. But I think part of the reason people don't experience it nowadays is because televisions are on in rooms and there's a lot more noise particularly in built-up areas. You wouldn't hear a car pull up anymore whereas older people would sit and listen to a clock.

I definitely believe it happened, 100 per cent. I wouldn't have believed it if she had died the following week. I'd have put it down to coincidence. I also know it couldn't have been a bird. It was three o'clock in the morning and birds don't fly at that time. It's also a low window with a shed close to it and I don't think a bird would come down at that angle.

Nor did it happen while we were waking up out of sleep. We were wide awake. Had we been awakened by the knocks I would have doubted we heard them. I would have thought it was a dream. You know the way, especially as a mother, you might think you heard a child fall out of bed? You are sure you heard it. But you listen and there's nothing. It's just you are half-way between waking and asleep. But we were wide awake and it definitely happened.

I don't know how it happens. Does it come from the person who is dying? If they are not yet dead, their spirit is still with them. So who gives the warning? I don't know. Yet it had to have come from her, from my granny.

It is also interesting that, especially with old people if you stay up with them as they are dying, if they get past three o'clock in the morning they generally live another day. There's something about three o'clock in the morning. Maybe your body is at a lower ebb, they reckon.

I think what happened is very reassuring because you feel

that there's more to life and you're going to see people again. I definitely think that there's something on the other side. I definitely think that the spirit leaves the body. And there's definitely a lot more that we don't know. If someone told us the story we might think, 'Well, there's *probably* such a thing.' But when you experience it yourself, you are convinced that there *definitely* is another world.

MARY, FROM COUNTY LOUTH, also heard tapping on her window prior to a tragedy that beset her family.

It was a Thursday night, back in 1977, and I was living in England. I was in my flat, which was three stories up. There was nobody else there but myself and my little child who was in bed. People had been up for coffee earlier but they had gone. I was clearing away the coffee cups. The next thing there was knocking on the window.

It was like the knuckles of a hand tapping on the window. It was like as if someone was rapping at the window-pane. It was just a couple of taps. When I heard it I wasn't afraid. I just went to the window to look. I thought to myself, 'I am three stories up. How could anyone be knocking on the window? You'd need a ladder to get up.'

There were no trees outside. It couldn't have been birds because it was late at night, about half-eleven. You wouldn't tend to get birds at that hour. And I never heard the sound before or since at that window. It was a once-off. I knew I was going to hear something from home or about a friend or somebody else. I just didn't realise how bad the news was that I was going to hear.

It was on the Thursday that I heard the knocking at the window. On the following Sunday I heard knocking at the door. I had some people up for dinner. I love to cook. I didn't have a dishwasher back then. I was washing up. The next thing there was a couple of raps at the front door.

One of my friends asked me, 'Do you hear that? Aren't you going to answer it?' I said, 'No.' I remember the person asking me, 'Why not?' I said, 'Because there's going to be nobody there.' He went to answer it. When he came back he said, 'There was nobody there!' People were looking at me like I was odd.

Then, on the following Thursday, I got the word that my two sisters and brother had died in a fire at home in Ireland. It wasn't a great surprise to me. Our family always had experienced things like this. There would be a knock at the door and there would be nobody there. After an event like that we knew that something was going to happen.

People really do think you are cracked when you say things like this. But I know what happened. At the time, though, even I thought it was really strange. I still don't know what it was but I wonder was it my grandmother, who I was really close to, coming back to warn me that something was going to happen. I just don't know. But I do really believe that there is something to it and something going on. I really do.

PATRICIA PLUNKETT, FROM COUNTY MAYO, had a similar forewarning of her uncle's death. Like the previous stories, it came in the form of knocking sounds.

I was very close to an uncle of mine who lived in England. We shared the same birthday and we were always very close. When I was a child he idolised me. After he went to England I used to go over every year to see him, as I grew up.

Unfortunately my uncle eventually died. He had been ill before Christmas. He had emphysema. On the day that he died his brother, who lives near me, phoned him and was talking to him for a full hour. He was in great form. We had no idea anything was wrong.

At 11.40 that night I was out in the kitchen trying to tune in a new television we had got that day. I was standing against the window. My husband was in bed because he had to get up early. I heard three bangs against the back door. The kids heard them too. They were saying, 'Who's here at this hour of the night?'

I thought, 'Oh, my God! Who could that be outside?' I didn't want to go out. I wasn't going to open the door myself. I just looked out the window and I turned on the outside light. The only thing I thought of is that someone might have had an accident outside and was looking for a telephone or whatever.

We had a dog at the time and he was standing looking at the back door. He was barking away. I said to one of the children, 'Go down and get Dad.' My husband came up, went out, walked around the house and there wasn't a sign of anybody. But the dog was still standing there, looking at the back door and barking. I thought, 'This is odd!'

Eventually the dog settled down. The kids went off to bed. And I went off to bed. However at 11.55 the dog started this unmerciful crying under my window. The dog never did that. It really was an unmerciful howl. I said, 'There's something wrong! Someone is going to die!' I said it to my husband. He said, 'I don't know what is wrong with that dog. I have never heard him cry like that.'

I was so upset I didn't sleep. I was waiting for someone to ring to tell me that my mother or father had died. They lived in the town on their own. But nothing happened. However, at seven o'clock the next morning, the phone rang. I said, 'This is it!' I got up and answered it. It was my mother on the phone. She said, 'Your uncle died last night.' He was her brother. He had died of a heart attack. I thought, 'My God! I don't believe it!'

I eventually went over to the funeral in Manchester. I was talking to my cousins about what happened that night. I told them about everything that occurred. They then told me it was 11.40 when he dropped on the floor and 11.55 when an ambulance had come. Unfortunately it was too late and he was declared dead. So I have absolutely no doubt it was him that night. He was coming to say goodbye.

THE HEART OF THE MATTER

Buddhists tell an interesting story about three men who got lost in the desert. The men became hot and thirsty. A large wall suddenly appeared before them. The first man climbed the wall and saw water and fertile land behind it. He jumped across. The second did the same. The third, however, acted differently. On observing the scene, he didn't cross over. Instead he returned to tell other desert wanderers about the paradise he had found.

Those who undergo near-death experiences have similarly viewed something amazing. Like the man in the desert, they have come back and described for us what they have seen. Many have encountered the central figure of world religions – the 'supreme being'. More have witnessed 'the light'. All have experienced the departure of the 'soul', 'spirit', 'mind' or 'consciousness' as it left their bodies for the afterlife.

Their extraordinary insights have almost certainly inspired and underpinned the world's many religions. Somewhere, way back in time, our forebears underwent near-death experiences resulting perhaps from a bad fall or a battle with a wild animal. They returned from the edge of death bearing images of bright lights, a wise being and meetings with deceased family and friends. Above all, they described an otherworld where we go when we die.

Various religions incorporated the stories they told. In certain faiths the 'supreme being' became known as God or

Allah. It was referred to as Vishnu, Krishna or Yahweh in others. Followers of Jesus Christ became Christians. More followed Islam, Judaism, Hinduism or any number of other additional creeds. It was a bit like a stained-glass window, where each fragment of glass produced a different colour. Behind the window was a single bright light – the ultimate source for the various colours or faiths.

The bright light has always been central. Most near-death survivors report it and value it. Once they witness it, they never want to leave it. The light is bliss, the origin of life and love, the core of everything that matters. Although intensely bright, even brighter than the sun, it doesn't dazzle. Either behind it, or in it, or close to it – or perhaps constituting the very light itself – is the 'supreme being', who is all-knowing, all-present and all-powerful. The being, neither a he nor a she, is understanding and kind.

Religions not surprisingly emphasise the light. Jesus tells us, 'I am the light of the world.' John begins his gospel, 'In Him was life, and the life was the light of men.' Psalm 27:1 proclaims, 'The Lord is my light and my salvation; whom shall I fear.' In Hinduism the Buddha is described as 'the enlightened one.' The prophet Muhammad is referred to as the 'light from Allah.' Sacred texts, it can be said, are bathed in light.

Judgements, or assessments of our life's deeds and misdeeds, figure too. Life reviews, as we have seen, are common during near-death experiences. They are also found in religions. 'I say unto you,' Matthew says in his gospel, 'that every idle word that men shall speak, they shall render an account for it in the day of judgement. For by thy words thou shalt be justified, and by thy words thou shalt be condemned.' John also takes up the theme, arguing that a person who believes in the eternal nature of God 'cometh not into judgement, but is passed from death to life.'

The soul is central as well. Those who undergo near-death experiences report how they leave their bodies and travel away. The process they describe is identical to what many religions believe is the soul or the spirit passing to eternal life. Ancient Egyptians believed that the soul, or *ka*, left the body and travelled to the afterlife. The great Greek philosopher Plato also believed in a 'soul' that lived on after bodily death. The Old Testament tells us how the soul or spirit 'shall return unto God who gave it.'

The concept of a 'soul' or 'spirit' independent of the body was intrinsic to the thinking of our forebears, the Celts, from the time of their arrival in Ireland some 600 years or so before Christ. There existed, they believed, another 'self' that survived death. This inner 'soul' or 'spirit' was immortal and indestructible and, having travelled to the otherworld, returned and was reincarnated in another form.

The Celts believed that our souls had a gathering place somewhere to the south-west of Ireland, on an island out into the sea. From there they were transported to the otherworld proper, possibly located in the raging ocean near where the sun sets in the west. Great mythical figures went to visit, including Cúchulainn and Oisín, the latter staying there some 300 years. Time, it was said, took on a different dimension in the land where our spirits resided.

The Celts felt closest to the spirit world around the time of Samhain, or 'summer's end', which was celebrated on 1 November. This date marked the transition between light and darkness, warmth and cold, the old and new years – a time when the harvest was in and the population settled down to a long and hard winter. It was also a time of greyness and shadows, when the borderline between the living and the dead became blurred.

On the eve of Samhain – 31 October – spirits, it was said, crossed the boundaries from the otherworld and they roamed throughout the earth. The dead returned to their homes. Foodstuffs, especially barley and milk, were put out in their honour. Doors were left open to allow them to revisit their former places of abode. Returning souls were asked for their help in predicting future events. Ancestral tales were recalled. This traditional 'night of the spirits' subsequently became Halloween.

In time, various religions subsumed these pagan traditions. Christian commemorations were superimposed over the pagan festivities. The Catholic Church gradually incorporated them into its calendar of events. The festival of the dead became the festivals of All Souls and All Saints. Prayers were offered for the souls of 'those departed' or for souls trapped in purgatory awaiting their entry to heaven.

Science, however, has never been – and may never be – impressed with talk of the soul or the spirit not to mention life after death or the near-death experience. To scientists, everything is explicable – the direct consequence of a vast network of nerve cells and molecules behaving in a particular way. Near-death experiences, scientists say, result from mass floods of endorphins or from oxygen deprivation. Visions are caused by complex electromagnetic fields. Premonitions are a by-product of chance.

Not every scientist agrees. 'Does the moon exist only when you look at it?' asked one scientist, who was unimpressed with the necessity of proof to establish ultimate truths. That scientist was Albert Einstein, the Nobel Prize winner who is often regarded as the father of modern physics. He believed that a different reality exists 'out there' whether we can observe it or explain it or not. Einstein's view, however, is not commonly or widely shared. We will turn our attention, therefore, to examining the store of scientific evidence that has been accumulated to date.

We will begin with the near-death experience. Many of the arguments and counter-arguments have already been assessed in *Going Home*, although some new ones have surfaced and I will deal with them shortly. The case for oxygen deprivation has previously been examined and dismissed. It is true that being deprived of oxygen is likely to cause hallucinations. However, it will also result in mental turmoil, agitation, disorientation and memory loss. The exact opposite occurs in the case of a near-death experience.

The position is similar with drugs. Some drugs generate hallucinations. But how can we explain cases that arise where people have taken no drugs at all? For example, many near-death experiences follow from an unexpected heart attack or a car crash or a near-drowning in a non-medical setting where no drugs are present. It has also been shown that patients who are given painkillers or anaesthetics have fewer and less-pronounced near-death experiences.

The case is also fragile when it comes to examining the role of endorphins. These are natural pain-killing chemicals which are released by the brain at times of stress. They cause a pain-free sense of bliss. But endorphins are also released at other stressful times in our lives and not just at the time of death. Why, then, don't those features associated with near-death experiences occur at times other than when facing death?

A further theory has surfaced since the writing of *Going Home* and it is worth examining in detail. The proposition is that near-death experiences may be caused by raised levels of carbon dioxide in the blood. This was the inference from a paper published by Slovenian scientists in April 2010. Their research study concluded that blood carbon dioxide levels were higher among cardiac arrest patients who reported near-death experiences than among those who did not. 'We can conclude,' said the report, 'that CO2 might be one of the major factors for provoking NDEs.'

The likely cause-and-effect mechanism is interesting and worth noting. We breathe in air containing oxygen and we breathe out air containing carbon dioxide. During a heart attack, a person may stop breathing. As a result, high levels of carbon dioxide build up in the bloodstream. The result might be hallucinations including bright lights and a few other characteristics of the near-death experience.

Once again, major problems exist. No sooner was the study published than it was pointed out that the presence of a high level of carbon dioxide is associated with a good resuscitation. And patients with good resuscitations tend to better remember their experiences. It is more likely, therefore, that survivors with high blood carbon dioxide levels merely have sharper memories of their near-death experiences and therefore have a greater tendency to recall them.

There are further potential flaws as well. For a start the sample size in the study was small, with only 11 out of 52 patients who were surveyed reporting near-death experiences. Other similar studies also contradict the Slovenian conclusions. One discovered that near-death experiences are linked to *below-average* carbon dioxide levels. Another found *no significant link at all*. Clearly, the connection remains tenuous.

Another more recent study concluded that near-death experiences may be caused by a surge of electrical energy released by the brain around the time of death. The research focused on seven critically-ill patients as they were released from life-support and died. The patients were linked up to electroencephalographs, which measure brain activity. In the hour or so before they passed away, brief but significant surges of electrical activity were observed, lasting from 30 – 180 seconds.

These cascades of electrical activity rippled through the dying brain in a manner not unlike an electrical storm. As they did so, they may have generated the sort of vivid mental sensations associated with the near-death experience. 'We speculate that in those patients who are successfully revived, they may recall the images and memories triggered by this cascade,' concluded the researcher, Dr. Lakhmir Chawla, an anaesthesiologist at George Washington University Medical Center in Washington D.C.

There are many major reservations associated with the study. For a start, although the research may have observed these electrical spikes, it failed to establish any connection whatsoever between them and the near-death experience. To put it quite simply, since all the people died we don't know what they were experiencing. The sample size – seven people – was also extremely small. Chawla additionally concluded: 'Our findings do not really tell us anything about whether there is an afterlife or not. Even if these near-death experiences turn out to be a purely biochemical event, there could still be a God.'

Returning to *Going Home*, the book also examined many possible explanations for the out-of-body component of the near-death experience. This sensation of floating outside one's body has major implications for the concept of life after death. The proposition that the soul or spirit can survive away from the body is essential to the existence of an afterlife. Otherwise, at best, we would just live on in our dead bodies. More likely we would not live on at all.

At the time of writing this book, a major study examining this issue is being coordinated by the University of Southampton.

The study involves 25 UK and USA hospitals and includes 1,500 patients. The approach is simple. Pictures are being placed on shelves high up in resuscitation areas. They can only be seen from the ceiling above. In the event that patients can accurately describe the pictures, the authenticity of the phenomenon will be established.

Researcher Dr. Sam Parnia, who heads up the study, has put it this way: 'If you can demonstrate that consciousness continues after the brain switches off, it allows for the possibility that the consciousness is a separate entity. It is unlikely that we will find many cases where this happens, but we have to be open-minded. And if no one sees the pictures, it shows these experiences are illusions or false memories.'

I wouldn't have high hopes for the study. To begin with, it is clear from those I have interviewed that the out-of-body journeys they go on are awesome and intense, involving extraordinary departures from their physical bodies and – in the case of near-death journeys – entailing travel to another world, bright lights, dark tunnels, encounters with dead relatives and meetings with 'God'. The last thing such people will get excited about is a picture near a hospital ceiling. They most likely won't notice it at all.

In addition, their experiences are clearly oriented more to 'feelings' and 'senses' than to physical observations. Those who return from near-death journeys say they 'sensed' meeting God but cannot necessarily come up with a description. Many also have 'felt' the warm familiarity of deceased relatives but can't put a face on them. Other images they describe, such as the shape and size of the border or boundary or even the tunnel, are often 'sensual' as well. The details contained in pictures below a ceiling – even for those undergoing a limited out-of-body experience – are unlikely to figure.

Further possible explanations were examined in *Going*

Home and I will mention two of them briefly. First there are dreams, which again don't seem to fit. Dreams, it has been well established, mostly occur during Rapid Eye Movement (REM) sleep. Out-of-body experiences, to the contrary, have been shown to be unconnected with REM sleep. Many also occur while the person is awake and not asleep at all. In addition, dreams are seldom recalled with anything like the same intensity.

Likewise, the proposal that near-death experiences are merely mirror-images of what happens at the time of birth is unconvincing. When we are born we travel through a birth canal, arrive into light and are greeted by welcoming faces. That is similar to the tunnel travel, bright light and meeting with relatives in a near-death experience. But what if someone was born through Caesarean section? Surely, in that case, there must be no tunnel as there was no birth-canal travel. Not so, concludes one study – tunnel travel occurs to almost the same extent in both cases.

Turning to visions and apparitions, the evidence is no more convincing or conclusive. One explanation put forward is that visions are subconscious dreams. Support for this theory derives, in the main, from the common observation that many visitations occur around the time of sleep. In particular, they often take place in the transition stage between sleeping and waking when the person is drowsy and the mind is calm and at ease. The majority occur in the relaxed atmosphere of the home – the perfect setting for dreaming.

The contrary proposition is that it is precisely in those circumstances that the mind is receptive to visitations from elsewhere. The absence of tension and stress helps create a relaxed, tranquil, meditative atmosphere which is conducive to experiencing supernormal events. That these events often occur perhaps in a comfortable bedroom at home is therefore far from surprising. Some experts also point out that, in any event, the visions are far from dreamlike and are normally described as 'vivid' and 'real.'

Another theory suggests that visions are nothing more than straightforward hallucinations that occur while conscious and awake. These hallucinations may be caused by a variety of factors, including schizophrenia. However, in the context of many of the cases we are concerned with – especially visions of the recently dead – the causes are more likely to be stress, sleep deprivation or emotional exhaustion.

It is easy to see how someone who is tired, troubled and worn out might imagine they had witnessed somebody close who had recently died. This may be even more understandable when the vision appears late at night, in a darkened room which is poorly lit and bathed in flickering shadows. As W. H. Salter – the eminent psychical researcher from the first half of the twentieth century – put it, 'Given poor light and a fit of nerves, how easy does a bush become a bear.'

This theory, however, is seriously undermined when the apparitional figure imparts information that was otherwise clearly unknown to the observer. Many cases are documented, including one involving psychiatrist Carl Jung. While in a dreamlike state following a friend's funeral, Jung was brought on a vivid tour through the deceased's library and directed by the dead person to a specific book. On checking later, Jung found the book – Emile Zola's *The Legacy Of The Dead* – in the location that was pinpointed. Jung had never before seen either the book or the library.

Perhaps the most compelling case ever recorded, where unknown information was imparted, was chronicled back in the 1920s by Sir William Barrett. The case, which featured in *Going Home* but is worth repeating, concerned a woman named Doris who was dying from heart failure following childbirth. 'Why, it's father! Oh, he's so glad I'm coming; he is so glad,' the woman exclaimed shortly before death. This was an obvious reference to her deceased father who was seemingly visible to her from her hospital bed.

Suddenly, with a puzzled expression, she exclaimed, 'He has Vida with him.' Once more she looked at her mother and said with incredulity: 'Vida is with him.' Vida was Doris's sister who had died more than two weeks earlier. Doris had not been made aware of the death. All information was kept from the woman because of her frail condition. Quite simply, she couldn't have known that Vida was dead.

Another theory proposes that those who see visions or apparitions possess what is often defined as a 'fantasy-prone personality'. The phrase was coined in the early 1980s by the American researchers Sheryl Wilson and Theodore Barber. The category covers people who not only fantasise frequently but who also tend to blur the dividing line between fantasy and reality. Their fantasies appear to them to be real. They account for an estimated four per cent of the population.

The 14 characteristics which the investigators Wilson and Barber linked to the fantasy-prone personality include having imaginary friends as a child, claiming psychic powers, being easily hypnotised, receiving special messages from spirits and experiencing waking dreams. Seeing visions is another characteristic. Fantasy-prone personalities also tend to have a wide collection of paranormal experiences.

While the proposition is compelling – and undoubtedly accounts for some vision reports – it is clearly restrictive. For a start, while it may explain *some* visions, it certainly fails to explain *all*. It is also argued that the category has become a 'dumping ground' for people who experience a reality that deviates from the norm. To merely explain away their experiences as the direct by-product of a propensity to fantasy is unsatisfactory, it is claimed.

An additional theory holds that electromagnetic fields can stimulate the brain in such a way that a person may see apparitions. The leading proponent of this idea is the Canada-based academic, author and psychologist Professor Michael Persinger. He argues that these fields – which are often associated with power lines, electrical devices and other complex technologies – may be far more prevalent in our living environment than suspected.

By stimulating certain parts of the brain with low-level electromagnetic fields, Persinger found that a number of characteristics associated with apparitions or hauntings could be replicated. Among those he listed were the experience of sensing a 'presence' and feelings of 'fear' or 'horror'. If the person is unaware that electromagnetic fields are the cause, which is most likely, they may automatically attribute the experience to the presence of a supernatural being such as a deceased relative or ghost.

Once again, the theory, while fascinating, has its deficiencies. For a start, the hallucinations that Persinger has replicated – including feelings of a 'presence' or sensations of fear – are vague and far-removed from the lifelike, well-defined, clear-cut apparitions described by people featured in this book and elsewhere.

Sceptics also question how the mechanism actually works – in particular how the low-level magnetic fields used in Persinger's studies can actually produce the sort of effects he describes. While it may well be the complexity of the electromagnetic fields and not just their amplitude that is important, the mechanism is unclear. Further independent, laboratory-based research work, sceptics argue, is required.

A final proposition worth looking at, regarding visions,

involves telepathy. The word strictly means 'distant experience' and involves the transfer of information from one person to another without the use of the five senses. In other words, hearing, sight, touch, smell and taste are not involved, either separately or collectively. Instead, some sort of 'sixth sense' is responsible for what occurs.

The possible role of telepathy was examined as far back as the late 1800s by the English psychologist and psychical researcher Edmund Gurney. From a series of experiments and studies, he concluded that a 'vision' is merely an image telepathically transferred by a dying person to another person some time before death occurs. The image is stored in the recipient's subconscious and surfaces at a later time. The impression is therefore created that the deceased has returned from the dead.

Things become a little more complicated for the telepathy theory when two or more people claim to witness the vision at the same time. This phenomenon of a number of witnesses simultaneously seeing the apparition was noted by Gurney. In this case, he argued, the main recipient of the vision telepathically passes the image to the others. It is, in other words, like a form of double telepathy, with the original image passing from the dying person to the main recipient and the main recipient relaying it to others.

Unfortunately for Gurney, his research conclusions have been seriously undermined in recent times. When compiling his studies he relied heavily on the assistance of the stage hypnotist, psychic and magic lantern lecturer George Albert Smith. A recent investigation has revealed that Smith faked many of the results which were used by Gurney in his research. This may have brought about Gurney's early death in 1888, at the age of 41, from a drug overdose in Brighton.

Despite this, telepathy remains a highly prominent area of investigation in explaining visions and apparitions.

As we saw earlier in this book, a minimum of one in ten people – representing some 600,000 Irish men, women and children, north and south of the border – will have seen or sensed an apparition or vision. That number, by any standards, is huge. One category, however, that almost certainly surpasses it involves premonitions, or the ability to foresee future events. While it is estimated that up to one-quarter of the population will report having a premonition, it is probably safe to say that almost everyone, at some stage or another, will have some sort of foreboding or presentiment, however small. Explaining them is just as perplexing as explaining visions.

One proposition put forward is that all of us, deep in our subconscious, have an innate ability to sense trouble ahead. This ability derives from an instinct or store of knowledge that, deep down inside, advises us of the safest paths to take. The 'intuitive warnings' we receive may never register on our conscious minds. They may instead rumble away under the surface. In doing so, they prompt us to avoid potentially calamitous events.

It has been noted, for example, how significantly fewer numbers of passengers book onto planes that crash. Only 22 per cent of seats were occupied on the Boeing 757 that crashed into the Pentagon on 9/11/2001. The occupancy rates for the planes that smashed into the North and South Towers of the World Trade Center were a mere 26 per cent and 19 per cent respectively. The average occupancy rate for all four tragic planes that day was an unusually low 21 per cent.

Similar results pertain in the case of the doomed *Titanic*. The White Star Line managed to fill only slightly more than one-half of the available passenger accommodation for its disastrous maiden voyage. At least 55 people – about four per cent of the total expected aboard – had a change of mind and cancelled. Professor Ian Stevenson, of the University of Virginia, documented 19 experiences relating to the *Titanic* which involved premonitions consisting mostly of general hunches or dreams.

We may ask: did potential passengers visualise trouble ahead? Perhaps they developed a 'gut feeling' that something was wrong? Maybe some subconscious trigger warned them to postpone their journeys or not travel at all? Or possibly, of course, the apparent cause-and-effect was the result of some sort of meaningless coincidence, chance aberration or false correlation.

Interestingly, this theme was taken up by the American researcher William Cox back in the 1950s. Using data for train crashes occurring from 1950 – 1955 he compared the occupancy rate on the day of each crash with rates for other days during the preceding week and on equivalent days in earlier weeks.

The results were remarkable. In one case alone, only nine passengers travelled on a train that crashed compared to a more typical complement numbering in the sixties. He concluded that, in all the cases he examined, less people travelled on the trains that crashed than on similar trains that didn't crash. The odds of this happening by chance were tiny.

Further research supports this idea that we can indeed see into the future. Some of the most fascinating studies were undertaken by the respected American researcher Dean Radin. His approach was simple yet brilliant. Volunteers were placed in front of a computer screen. Once they pressed a mouse, the screen produced either a calm image or an emotional image. Calm images included landscapes and happy people. Emotional images included erotic scenes and autopsies.

The volunteers were hooked up to sensors measuring heart rate and sweating, among other indicators of arousal. Once they pressed the mouse, the computer screen stayed blank for five seconds. Then, either a calm image or an emotional image – randomly selected by the computer – showed up on the screen. This process was repeated over and over again.

Predictably, over the tense five seconds that the volunteers waited for the image to appear, indicators showed that their arousal increased in anticipation of what they were about to see. That was exactly what the research team expected. What surprised them, however, was that the level of arousal *increased by an even greater amount* before an emotional picture showed. Incredibly, the volunteers were accurately predicting what sort of picture was about to appear not only before it was shown but even before the computer had randomly selected it. They were, in other words, accurately predicting future events.

There have been many proposals put forward as to why behaviour patterns such as these might occur. One of the most notable originated from the extraordinary brain of Irishman John William Dunne, who was born in County Kildare in 1875. Dunne was, quite literally, a 'dreamer'. He dreamt, with uncanny accuracy, of the violent eruption of Mount Pelée, Martinique, in 1902. He dreamt of a tragic factory fire in Paris. He once even dreamt that his watch had stopped at a particular time only to discover on awakening that indeed it had.

Intrigued by these strange forewarnings, Dunne turned his attention to explaining them. The answer, he concluded, lies in the nature of time. Peculiarly, he noted, some of his dreams reviewed events from the past while others foresaw events from the future. How could it be, he wondered, that our minds seem to flit across the past and the future while in a dreaming state but only focus on the present while we are awake?

The reason, Dunne postulated, is that the past, present and future all happen together and are part of a unified reality. All time is eternally present. It is only in sleep, however, that the mind wanders freely. Only then can we drift through the past, present and future with carefree abandon. While awake, in sharp contrast, the mind interprets time in a linear, one-directional fashion.

Dunne suggested that we can best understand what occurs by imagining we are playing a piano. In the awakened state we play the piano keys one after another in sequence, from left to right. Our hand travels in only one direction, note after note. By way of contrast, while asleep we become virtuosos, flashing to and fro across the keyboard, moving all over the piano and interpreting the full span of keys at will.

Lest we dismiss Dunne as some sort of quaint eccentric, espousing outlandish and laughable views, it is worth noting that he became one of the most highly-respected thinkers of his time. Not only was he an aeronautical engineer and inventor of international renown but his work on dreams and his theories on time were well-received. Authors J. B. Priestley and Aldous Huxley ranked among his admirers. He died in 1949.

My own impressions of the 'otherworld' derive entirely from my conversations with those who have 'been there' and come back. Over a period of three years I have spoken with numerous people from all walks of life who have had near-death experiences – men and women, young and old, rich and poor, atheists and believers representing the Roman Catholic, Presbyterian, Methodist, Church of Ireland and Hindu faiths, among others. The common ground evident in their stories is remarkable.

The otherworld they experience seems to be one of the senses. Although not a physical world, images are sometimes described in a physical way. For example, a few automatically interpret the 'supreme being' they meet as being 'Jesus'. Sometimes, in the blue or white light, they claim to have seen 'Mary' or 'Our Lady'. But these, it seems, are mostly real-life interpretations they put on the figure they encounter, to help establish its status, standing and importance.

While the vast majority can't describe the being's physical characteristics, they 'feel' and 'perceive' that it is intelligent, kind, compassionate and all-powerful. They are 'sure' it is the person we regard as God. Their knowledge is sensual. It is often only following pressure from me to describe what the being looks like – and that pressure I deliberately apply to see where it leads – that they succumb and describe some well-known religious figure or perhaps even 'a person in white robes, with a beard.'

Many other impressions are sensual as well. For example, my interviewees almost invariably describe feelings of warmth, peace, serenity, tranquillity or happiness while travelling to the other side. These senses or feelings are paramount. Those I speak to often have an overwhelming compulsion to cross over because they 'perceive' that what is ahead is the ultimate destination. They 'know' it is a good place to go to. They 'feel' they are 'going home'.

Many also have a sense that they 'know' the relatives or friends who come to greet them – and are delighted to meet them – but they can't always describe who they are or what they are like. This is contrary to our automatic imagining of our deceased in the otherworld dressed in familiar clothes or with customary features. Once again, the world the relatives or friends emerge from is a world of the senses although people I talk to may often translate what they see into images understandable in earthly terms.

Time also takes on a different dimension in this faraway place. For many, the complete experience – from the tunnel travel right through to the return – occurs in perhaps 20 or 30 seconds. This may be the extent of time they were later deemed to be medically dead. One woman, who also had a life review, went through a lengthy series of images and evaluations, yet when she returned to real life she was still being wheeled down the same hospital corridor where, just seconds before, she had first left her body.

Knowledge, or great perception, is also reported by many. I was struck by the intense understanding and profound insights that are often gleaned in the process of passing over. Fundamental truths come to be known. Unfortunately many of these divinations or principles or axioms are lost or forgotten on return to earthly life. Those who come back are annoyed that they cannot recall them and over long periods of time regret their loss.

There is, however, one fundamental truth almost all bring back. That truth is 'love'. This is not the love of lust or attachment. No animal instinct or flood of bodily chemicals can explain it. Nor is it self-centred or self-seeking. Gain is never an objective. Instead it is a heart-focused feeling of universal love involving caring for others, being kind and respectful, and showing concern for the welfare and feelings of fellow human beings.

It is a love that is charitable, altruistic and unconditional. Generous and forgiving, it is directed at all people and not just a select few. It is also intense. Those who return are sometimes overwhelmed by it and struggle to explain it because of its vastness and profundity. They often say it is beyond worldly description. It is also, they insist, the key to life and our passport to a happy death and a good passage to the other side.

Most survivors refer to it. Actor Larry Hagman, following his near-death experience, talked of 'love' being the main feature of the 'collective energy' that surrounds us all. 'It's with us now, it always has been, and it always will be,' he reflected. Another actor, Peter Sellers, after his near-death journey in 1964, again spoke of love. 'I knew there was love, real love, on the other side of the light which was attracting me so much. It was kind and loving and I remember thinking, "That's God,"' he said.

Love's central importance has been noted by virtually all the researchers who have examined the near-death experience. Dr. Raymond Moody – who was the original chronicler of the phenomenon back in 1975 – observed it. Another well-known researcher, P. M. H. Atwater, commented on it too. She said: 'I have always been impressed that, once you peel away the research data and everyone's opinion about the stories, what remains is really all about love.'

We should not be surprised, by now, to discover that a carbon-copy concept of love appears in most world religions. References to it are everywhere to be found. 'God is love,' John declares in his first epistle. 'Love your neighbour as yourself,' Jesus instructs. 'Love is patient. Love is kind. It does not envy. It does not boast. It is not proud,' Paul advises in one of his epistles. Other religions, including Islam, Buddhism and Hinduism, are suffused with the concept of 'love'.

My interviewees also emphasised its importance. 'Love is behind it all. That really is it. We are all part of the spirit of love. That is what I learned,' remarked Paula, from County Waterford, who was featured earlier in this book. 'It's not just a case of getting by each day and acquiring as much as we can. Physical stuff means nothing. What matters is the way you are with yourself and with others, your honesty and kindness, and the way you treat other people.'

Love – along with its associated qualities of benevolence and goodness to others – also constitutes the standard by which we are judged during the life review. A woman who experienced one, Monica, from County Limerick, outlined her views in *Going Home*. 'The experience has changed my life,' she reflected. 'It lives on with me and hopefully has made me a more compassionate, caring person. I turn the other cheek and people will even remark to me that I would be nice to people that maybe wouldn't be nice to me. But I do it because I know that someday everything I do and say in this life will be reviewed by me again.'

Charles, from County Roscommon, who was judged, or assessed, during an experience he had while being operated on, had this to say in a previous chapter: 'I rarely go to mass or confession. I used to but I got out of it and a couple of years after the operation I stopped going to church. I don't think it matters. But it does matter to be a good person. That's what I think is important. When people talk about death, that's when I think about it. And I tell them if they have a good life there's nothing to fear.'

Sam, who comes originally from Derry, adds that the only thing we can do is our best. 'What also came across was that you didn't have to be perfect in life,' he concluded following his judgement. 'That was clear when I was told, "You haven't done too bad! You've done OK!" In other words I didn't do too badly on earth. It was about doing your best. You don't have to be a "Holy Joe". "You tried, therefore you are OK" was the message.'

It appears, therefore, that the proponents of 'love' down through the ages were ultimately right. The Beatles' 'All You Need Is Love' was remarkably prescient, expressing a truth spanning time. Equally perceptive was Virgil, writing in the century before Christ, who said, 'Love conquers all.' Or the apostle John, who wrote in the century after Christ, 'God is love.' Or any number of those who, through their near-death experiences, have witnessed the power of love in the light.

'Without love I am nothing,' Paul declared in his first epistle to the Corinthians. It is the ineffable truth to which those who have returned ascribe. Compassion, kindness and a sense of humanity towards others are the supreme benchmark. Coldness, cruelty, meanness and indifference define darkness. These rules, say those who have witnessed the light, are the ultimate key to the kingdom and the passport for all of us on our journeys to the other side.

ACKNOWLEDGEMENTS

I am most grateful to all those people who contacted me following the publication of *Going Home* in late 2009. Their interest was appreciated, their support valued, their kindness heart-warming, their stories remarkable. Without their input, and the input of all the other case histories, this book would never have been written.

I owe particular thanks to a number of radio programmes for prompting people to get in touch. Among the most helpful were Weeshie Fogarty's *In Conversation With . . .* on Radio Kerry, Gerry Kelly's afternoon show on LMFM along with Joe Nash's morning show on Limerick's Live95FM.

The Morning Show on TV3 and Joe Duffy's *Spirit Level* on RTÉ were also of immense assistance, as were Ryan Tubridy's and Pat Kenny's shows on RTÉ Radio 1. I am additionally indebted to Wendy Austin and her team at *Talkback* on BBC Radio Ulster, not to mention Community Radio Youghal.

Numerous other radio stations assisted, in one way or another, including Newstalk, Dublin's 98FM, Lyric FM, Clare FM, Downtown Radio, South East Radio, BBC Radio Foyle, Tipp FM, WLR FM, Cork 96FM, Shannonside FM, Midwest Radio, Dundalk FM, Galway Bay FM, KFM and East Coast FM in County Wicklow.

My gratitude also to the editors of *Ireland's Own*, *Belfast Telegraph*, *Irish News*, *Waterford Today*, *Connacht Tribune* and *Irish Catholic*, who published letters seeking help. Their support was invaluable. Additional thanks to Cree's and to the Ailbrin Society in Youghal, County Cork, for the special events that introduced me to some remarkable stories.

There are many excellent and helpful books on the near-death experience which I would like to recommend. Among them are *Life After Life* and *The Light Beyond* by Dr. Raymond Moody, *The Truth In The Light* by Dr. Peter Fenwick and Elizabeth Fenwick, *Closer To The Light* by Dr. Melvin Morse, *Dying To Live* by Dr. Susan Blackmore and *Death's Door* by Jean Ritchie.

Also of interest are *The Return From Silence* by D. Scott Rogo, *The Case For Heaven* and *Glimpses Of Heaven* by Mally Cox-Chapman and two books by P. M. H. Atwater – her excellent *Beyond The Light* and her comprehensive *The Big Book Of Near-Death Experiences*.

On the visions front, *Beyond The Threshold* by Dr. Christopher Moreman, *Is There An Afterlife?* by David Fontana and *Parting Visions* by Dr. Melvin Morse with Paul Perry are all excellent works. So also, of course, are the iconic *Death-Bed Visions* by Sir William Barrett and *The Peak In Darien* by Frances Power Cobbe.

Dr. Carla Wills-Brandon's *One Last Hug Before I Go* and Bill and Judy Guggenheim's *Hello From Heaven!* are other worthwhile reads. The same can also be said, concerning premonitions, for Dr. Larry Dossey's excellent *The Power Of Premonitions*, which is a classic in its field.

Lastly, regarding books, I am indebted to a number of autobiographies for accounts of the near-death experiences or visions of international celebrities. Among them are actor Larry Hagman's *Hello Darlin'*, rock 'n' roll star Tommy Steele's *Bermondsey Boy*, singer Tony Bennett's *The Good Life* and actor Micheál Mac Liammóir's *All For Hecuba*. Equally valuable was the autobiography of psychiatrist Carl Jung, *Memories, Dreams, Reflections*.

A number of individuals also deserve credit and I will mention them briefly. Kathleen O'Connor was pleasantly forthcoming with her comments regarding the cover. Kay Healy, from County Wicklow, led me to some fascinating interviewees. John Kennedy, from County Cork, was ever helpful. I am also thankful to James Plunkett-Coyle, who introduced me to one of the most moving stories in the book.

Linda Monahan, from Typeform, was her usual excellent self in designing the cover and was, needless to say, a pleasure to deal with. Typeform's Pat Conneely also did commendable work laying out the text, while Roy Thewlis was always obliging. My thanks also go to the staff at ColourBooks, especially Gerry Kelly.

The death of my brother-in-law, Alex Fitzgerald, occurred as this book came to fruition. It could never be said that Alex was a profound believer, although his decency and moral sense were widely regarded. Yet, shortly before he passed on, he reached out his arms, focused his eyes on the far horizon and smiled as if in contact with those who had already passed over. His place in a better world is guaranteed.

Finally, and not for the first time, I would like to thank Úna O'Hagan for her help during all stages of this book. Although she would never admit it, she was in every way co-producer of this project from its initial conception right through to its arrival on bookshop shelves and beyond. She played a central role in helping to achieve what the book set out to accomplish – namely, establishing what faces us all on arrival at 'the distant shore'.